# The Search for Fulfillment

## (Part 1)

### Understanding your God given needs
### and the search to fulfill them

by

## Timothy Williams

Printed in the United States: Third printing

ISBN: 978-1511584739

The Lord's Sentinel Publishing House
P.O. Box 44
Lake Placid, Fl 33862

# Table of Contents

## Part 1 (Book 1)

Chapters

## Part 2 (Book 2)

Chapters

5- The Search for Love

6- The Search for Maturity

7- The Search for Humility

8- The Search for Self Worth

## Part 3 (Book 3)

Chapters

9- The Search for Freedom (part 1)

10- The Search for Freedom (part 2)

11- The Search for Endurance

12- The Search for God

# Selected Bibliography (by author)

Baker, John- Celebrate Recovery

Blackaby, Henry- Experiencing God

Cloud, Henry and Townshend, John- False Assumptions, How People Grow

Collins, Gary- The Biblical Basis of Christian Counseling for People Helpers

Cowman, L.B.- Streams in the Desert

Crabb, Larry- Basic Principles of Biblical Counseling, Effective Biblical Counseling, Shattered Dreams, Connecting

Eareckson-Tada, Joni- When God Weeps: Why Our Sufferings Matter to the Almighty, Heaven: Your Real Home

Foster, Richard- Celebration of Discipline, Prayer

Frankl, Viktor- Man's Search for Meaning

Frost, Jack- Experiencing Father's Embrace, From Slavery to Sonship, Breaking Free (Exposing Bitter Root Strongholds)

Jeremiah, David- Slaying the Giants in Your Life

Lee, Jimmy Ray and Strickland, Dan- Living Free

Maxwell, John- Today Matters, Be All You Can Be, Success One Day at a Time, The Winning Attitude, 21 Laws of Leadership, The 360 Degree Leader

McGee, Robert- The Search for Significance (video and book)

Robertson, Norman- Winners in Christ

Shields, Harry and Bredfeldt, Gary- Caring for Souls

Ten Boom, Corrie- The Hiding Place

Warren, Rick- Purpose Driven Life

Wilkinson, Bruce- Secrets of the Vine, Prayer of Jabez

# Selected Bibliography (reference books by title)

Analytical Greek New Testament (Friberg-Friberg)
Complete Word Study Dictionary, New Testament (Zodhiates)
Englishman's Greek Concordance and Lexicon (Wigram-Green)
Englishman's Hebrew/Aramaic Concordance (Wigram-Green)
Evangelical Dictionary of Theology (EDT; Elwell)
Greek-English Lexicon, abridged (LSJa; Liddell-Scott-Jones)
Greek-English Lexicon (BAGD; Bauer-Arndt- Gingrich-Danker)
Hebrew English Lexicon (BDB; Brown-Driver-Briggs-Gesenius)
Interlinear Greek-English New Testament (Green)
King James Version (KJV)
NASB-NIV Parallel NT in Greek and English (Marshall)
New American Standard Bible (NASB)
New Bible Dictionary (NBD; Douglas)
New International Dictionary of NT Theology (NIDNTT; Brown)
New International Version (NIV)
New King James Version (NKJV)
New Revised Standard Version (NRSV)
Renewal Theology (Williams)
Septuagint with Apocrypha: Greek and English (LXX; Brenton)
Strong's Concordance and Dictionary (SC)
Theological Dictionary of the New Testament, abridged (TDNTa; Kittel-Friedrich-Bromiley)
Theological Dictionary of the OT (TDOT; Botterweck)
Theological Wordbook of the OT (TWOT; Harris-Archer-Waltke)
Topical Analysis of the Bible (TAB; Elwell)
Vine's Expository Dictionary of Biblical Words (Vine-Unger-White)
Vocabulary of the Greek Testament (MM; Moulton-Milligan)
Webster's New Twentieth Century Dictionary
Word Studies in the New Testament (Vincent)
Wuest's Word Studies from the Greek New Testament (Wuest)
Zondervan Pictorial Encyclopedia of the Bible (ZPEB; Tenney)

# About the Author

Tim Williams earned his masters degree in Biblical studies from Regent University (Virginia Beach, Virginia), where he studied theology under J. Rodman Williams, Owen Weston, and Jon Ruthven. He later earned his masters degree in counseling from Palm Beach Atlantic University. He is the author of four books- *The Spiritual Gifts (Part 1): The Ascension Gifts of Christ and the Functional Gifts of God*; and *The Spiritual Gifts (Part 2): The Gifts of the Holy Spirit*; and *The Reconciliation of 1Timothy 2:11-15 with Galatians 3:26-28 in the Context of Women in Ministry: An Eschatological Tension;* and *The Battle to Fulfill your Destiny in God* (with Juanita Folsom). He also has written a Christian counseling curriculum- *Soul Care Ministry*. His ministry focus is teaching and one-on-one counseling (with inner healing) that is Christ centered and Holy Spirit directed. He has worked as a therapist for incarcerated youth and is presently serving as a Christian counselor in Sebring, Florida.

# Introduction

Meaning, purpose, love, happiness- these are things that everyone is searching for. When we find these things, we find fulfillment. We have certain deep needs of the soul that are God given, and we diligently search to meet these needs in order to find fulfillment and to be happy. We must find meaning, purpose, achievement, love, meaningful relationships, maturity, humility, self worth, significance, freedom, endurance, and God. These are the things that give us fulfillment and hope for the future.

We are driven to find fulfillment and happiness in life, and we will do whatever we think will make us happy and fulfilled. There is great pain if you do not find fulfillment or life has no meaning or you cannot find purpose and love. The greatest pain is not finding fulfillment and happiness and believing that you will never have this. You can even be living for God and still not find the fulfillment you are looking for. This is why many people do not care about living anymore and why some people even try to kill themselves.

In *The Search for Fulfillment* the author shares the brokenness in his own life that led him to learn how we find fulfillment. If you are directionless or unmotivated or stuck in life or unsatisfied or angry or troubled or hurting or brokenhearted or discouraged about your life, even to the point where you want to quit trying (and even to the point of not wanting to live anymore), this book is for you.

This work has been divided into three parts in order to make reading easier. Each chapter can be read apart from the others and in no set order, although it is beneficial to read chapter one first for the author's story.

**Part I** consists of chapters one through four. **Chapter one** is the introduction to the search for **Fulfillment**. It gives the premise for why we search for fulfillment, that we have God given needs that must be met in order to find fulfillment. It also describes the author's experience that compelled him to write this book. **Chapter two** is the search for **Meaning**. You find meaning by living for a cause greater than you and living for someone who is dear to you. Let this someone and cause be God and the gospel of Jesus Christ. You also find meaning by feeling connected to your world through loving God and others and having the hope of life after death that is better than this life. You must find meaning in suffering or your life has no meaning, and you will find meaning by what you are willing to suffer for. **Chapter three** is the search for **Purpose**. You find purpose by putting into action how you will give yourself to a cause greater than you and how you will live for someone who is dearest to you. This purpose is activated by losing your life for Jesus Christ. You also find general purpose through fulfilling work (achievement), meaningful relationships (love), and self improvement (maturity), but these will be discussed in separate chapters. **Chapter four** is the search for **Achievement**. You find achievement by having fulfilling work and achieving goals and believing that you are doing work that is useful and benefits others and has lasting purpose. We find purpose through fulfilling work, and fulfilling work can be found in ministry, vocation, or volunteer service, but everyone has spiritual gifts and is called to ministry.

Part II consists of chapters five through eight. **Chapter five** is the search for **Love**. You find love by having meaningful relationships and belonging to a family where you can find acceptance, affirmation, friendship, and security, and you must love God and others and be at rest in the Father's love. **Chapter six** is the search for **Maturity**. You find maturity by becoming a better person (and becoming more like Christ) through improving your character and developing your talents and reaching your full potential, and this comes forth primarily through discipline. **Chapter seven** is the search for **Humility**. You find humility by losing pride and self centeredness and recognizing your spiritual poverty before God, and humility must be developed by getting principles of humility into your heart, practicing these principles, and being willing to be trained in humility. **Chapter eight** is the search for **Self Worth**. You find self worth by believing that you are a loveable, valued, and competent individual who is created in the image of God and that your life matters and has significance. The foundation for self worth is being a son of God, which comes forth by being justified before God through faith in Jesus Christ.

**Part III** consists of chapters nine through twelve. **Chapter nine** is the search for **Freedom** (part 1), which is freedom of the heart. You find freedom by resolving pain, bitterness, and judgments. This chapter defines pain, bitterness, and judgments and helps you identify the pain, bitterness, and judgments in you. **Chapter ten** is the continuation of the search for **Freedom** (part 2). This chapter explains the spiritual weapons and the steps for resolving pain, bitterness, and judgments. For serious trauma and hurt, there is also trauma therapy and inner healing. It also offers help for anger, guilt, depression, fear, anxiety, and problem thoughts. **Chapter eleven** is the search for **Endurance**. You find endurance by persevering in righteousness with a positive attitude through tribulation and the hardships of life. The result is that you develop greater strength and faith for today and tomorrow and have hope for a better future. **Chapter twelve** is the search for **God**. The search for God is seeking God. You grow spiritually and experience God and know God better when you seek God. The author offers advice from Scripture and personal experience for how God changes and renews us and how we can know the voice of God and be able to know the will of God. The **Epilogue** affirms that these searches are God given needs and that fulfilling these needs helps you fulfill the will of God for your life and your destiny in God. There is a final challenge to the reader to seek God in order to find change and greater fulfillment.

# Chapter 1

# The Search for Fulfillment

Meaning, purpose, love, happiness- these are things that everyone is searching for. When we find these things, we find fulfillment. Fulfillment is finding fullness, filling up what was empty or lacking in one's soul. Thus, fulfillment has connotations of depth. It signifies something that is deep as opposed to happiness, which can imply an emotion that is superficial or shallow or fleeting or temporary. Happiness might be a more popular and well used word than fulfillment, but fulfillment has been chosen because it speaks of depth (although happiness will be used as a synonym at times). When we are fulfilled, we are more than happy, for we have found contentment and satisfaction deep down in our soul.

Fulfillment comes by meeting the deep needs of the soul. We have certain deep needs of the soul, and we diligently search to meet these needs in order to find fulfillment and to be happy. We must find meaning, purpose, achievement, fulfilling work, success, love, meaningful relationships, maturity, humility, self worth, significance, freedom, endurance, and spirituality. These are the things that give us fulfillment.

We are driven to find fulfillment and happiness in life, and we will do whatever we think will make us happy and fulfilled. There is great pain if you do not find fulfillment or if life has no meaning for you, especially if you cannot find purpose and love. The greatest pain in the world is to never find fulfillment and happiness and to believe that you will never find fulfillment and happiness. This is why many people do not care about living anymore and why some people even try to kill themselves.

We see people committing suicide or dying of an overdose of drugs. We even see famous people committing suicide. These famous people have attained fame and fortune, and we wonder

11

why they would do such a thing, but they apparently had so much inner pain that they could not find fulfillment and their life had no meaning. You try to kill yourself when you hate your life and your life has become meaningless and you have absolutely no hope for a better future, no hope that you will ever find fulfillment and happiness. Depression can drive you to these negative emotions, but depression in itself does not drive you to kill yourself.[1]

The search for fulfillment is probably the most important truth for understanding human psychology. It has been said that when people live poorly, it is because they are not finding fulfillment or life has no meaning for them. When you cannot find fulfillment or meaning, if you cannot find a certain measure of happiness, there is tremendous pain and emptiness, and you are driven to ease this pain and fill this emptiness by looking for some type of comfort. You might be driven into pleasure seeking, withdrawal and fantasy, aggressive striving in work and activities, addictions, substance use, or even trying to kill yourself.

If you cannot find fulfillment, life becomes a burden to bear rather than an experience to enjoy, and you will battle emptiness every day of your life. And you wonder why you are always feeling angry, bitter, anxious, lonely, guilty, or depressed. You wonder why you are compelled to work too much or are not motivated to work at all. You wonder why you aggressively strive in your responsibilities or are afraid of having responsibilities. It is because you are not finding fulfillment and happiness.

If you lose hope of ever finding fulfillment, believing that you will never be happy or successful or never be free from pain and emptiness, hopelessness and despair will grip your heart so that you will see no reason for living anymore. You will see no purpose in life. This inner pain will become unbearable, and the trials and tribulations of life will begin to overwhelm you so that even the smallest problem becomes a mountain too great to climb. You will reach the place where you hate your life and wonder what life really means in the midst of all this pain. You must find fulfillment if you hope to enjoy life and have the ability to cope with stress and have the strength to face your problems.

---

1- Robin Williams recently committed suicide (at the writing of this chapter). He made us laugh, but apparently he could not find happiness and fulfillment.

We have certain deep needs of the soul, and these needs become the great searches of the human soul. We will search to fill this need or, if we do not see the need, we will search to find something that will make us happy or give us pleasure or comfort. This book identifies ten of these needs, identifies some principles for meeting these needs, and shows how God is the center and foundation of every need. These needs are briefly described below.

We must find meaning in life. You find meaning by giving yourself to a cause and a person greater than you and feeling connected to your world and having hope of life after death.

We must find purpose in life. You find purpose by dying to yourself in order to live for this cause and person and building this kingdom. You also find purpose by finding fulfilling work and meaningful relationships and becoming a better person.

We must find achievement. You find achievement by having fulfilling work, being successful, achieving goals, and believing that you are doing work that is useful and has lasting purpose.

We must find love, to love and to be loved. You find love by having meaningful relationships and belonging to a family where you can find acceptance and security.

We must find maturity. You find maturity by changing and becoming a better person through improving your character and developing your talents so that you can reach your full potential.

We must find humility. You find humility by losing pride and self centeredness and recognizing your spiritual poverty before God and trusting God.

We must find self worth. You find self worth by believing that you are a loveable, valued, and competent individual who has the ability and courage to do good and that your life has significance.

We must find freedom (freedom of the heart). You find freedom by resolving pain and bitterness and not being bound by anger, fear, anxiety, worry, guilt, or depression.

We must find endurance. You find endurance by persevering in righteousness with a positive attitude through suffering, tribulation, and the hardships of life so that you develop faith for today and hope for the future.

We must find the spiritual realm and believe in God and seek God (the search for God). You must seek God in order to grow spiritually and experience God, and God must be the center and foundation for all your searches. You will seek God when you see that there is something more than this life.

These are the needs that every human being has, and we must meet these needs in order to find fulfillment. It does not matter if you do not see them or misidentify them. These needs are there and they will drive your emotions and cause you to search for fulfillment and happiness. You will either search to fulfill a need or search to find something that will ease the pain or fill the emptiness that is being caused by this unmet need.

I believe that the primary goal for every human being is to be happy. We know that we want to be happy and have fun and enjoy life, and so we go out and pursue what we think will make us happy, maybe looking for pleasure, excitement, self improvement, love, or money to find satisfaction. We just want to be happy and will search for what we think will make us happy. We might focus on finding love and getting married and having a family. We might focus on exercise or outdoor activities. We might focus on getting an education and a career that we believe will fulfill us. We might focus on being successful and making money so that we will have financial security. We might pursue a job or an activity where we can help people and feel that we are making a difference in this world. We might find a certain measure of happiness in these things, but deep down inside we feel that there must be more to life than this, and when we are near or at retirement, we might ask, "What was life all about?"

Thus, in the midst of trying to find happiness and fulfillment, and even when you find some measure of fulfillment and happiness, you might still sense emptiness in your heart and a lack of fulfillment, even though you are not able to identify the cause. You might feel stuck in life and feel that life is leaving you behind. You might have attained your goals but have a desire for something more. You might experience boredom or loneliness and desperately want change. You might have experienced failure and a lack of success to the point where you are hurting and may feel that you are not good enough. You might have tried to meet a need, but the search to fulfill this need has been fruitless. You might come to a place where your dreams, goals, and expectations about life have not been fulfilled and you are getting old, and if you believe in God, you may even feel that God has let you down.

This is the place where you might find yourself, and you wonder how you can get out of this pit. You look for ways to change your life. You might think that getting a new job or a new spouse or a new career or a new hobby is the answer. If you have faith in God, you might think that waiting for God to do something is the answer. You may even be at the place where you are desperate for change or desperate to find happiness and fulfillment or desperate to find comfort or pleasure to ease the inner pain.

When we search for fulfillment and happiness or when we search to fill the emptiness or to ease the pain, this is when we are susceptible to making wrong choices and bad decisions. This is when we are in a very vulnerable position and can easily fall into a trap. When you are in this place, you must be very careful and be led by wisdom and truth and not emotions and desires. This is being led by the Spirit of God and not the flesh. If we are led by our emotions and desires, we will be enticed by temptation and fall into a trap and get ourselves into trouble. This is usually how we get into sin and experience failure.

When people sin or fail, the counseling perspective of the Church has been to focus on the sin or the failure. There may be the ministry of grace and forgiveness, but if there is a root to the problem and this root is not removed, the person will fall into temptation again. When we sin or fail, it is usually because we are trying to find fulfillment or happiness in what is not good for us and is not the will of God, and so we fall into a trap. This trap of the enemy is a temptation that is built upon your desire to be happy or the emptiness or pain that you are feeling (and may even be speaking). We fall for this trap because we believe that a certain person, place, or activity will make us happy or take away the emptiness and pain and give us fulfillment.

When we sin or fail because we are searching for happiness or trying to fill some kind of emptiness or to ease an inner pain, if this issue is not resolved, you will continue falling into traps, always needing grace and forgiveness but never finding success and victory. I want to find success and victory. The grace of God is a given for the penitent person, but there are consequences for your actions. Therefore, I want to know how to be successful and have victory. We must find fulfillment if we hope to have success and victory in life, even if it is only discovering a new perspective.

I believe very strongly that the cause for many problems, even for Christians, is that we are not finding fulfillment in life. This is a belief that is held by many leading Christian counselors. There is a hidden truth in the Church that most people would never believe or understand. It is this: You can be born of the Spirit and filled with the Spirit and anointed in the gifts of the Spirit and be serving and loving God, and still not find fulfillment. We can see this today in the Church, even in the pulpit, where so many leaders are resigning from the ministry because they have failed or burned out.

The Christian counseling profession has tried to make the issue to be about sin without getting at underlying issues. I believe in sin. If you do not believe in the sin nature, you do not know the first thing about human nature. We are sinners and anything that falls short of the glory of God can be called sin. The problem about sin, however, is how the concept of sin is applied.

Many Christian counselors practice what is called Nouthetic counseling, which comes from a Greek word that means to admonish.[2] This counseling perspective says that if there is something dysfunctional in your life, you must be doing something wrong, you must be violating the Word of God. The objective is to find the sin (to find what you are doing wrong), give appropriate Scriptures for correction, and admonish you to stop doing it and obey the Word of God (and this is why it is called admonishing).[3]

While sin can be defined as missing the mark or not being perfect, which means that anything short of perfection can be defined as sin, this focus on finding the sin can be deceptive and can easily get you on the wrong track for at least two reasons. First, there may be an underlying issue that needs to be addressed before a sin can be overcome. If the underlying issue is emptiness or inner pain or a lack of fulfillment and this is not dealt with, the

---

2- The Greek word is *noutheteo* (SC-#3560, verb), which means "to admonish, reprove, remind" (Acts 20:31, Rom 15:14, 1Cor 4:14, Col 1:28, 3:16, 1Thes 5:12,14, 2Thes 3:15). The corresponding noun is *nouthesia* (SC-#3559), which means "admonishment" (1Cor 10:11, Eph 6:4, Titus 3:10).

3- This has also been called Biblical counseling, but there are many kinds of Biblical and Christian counseling. While this is a valid counseling method, it is only one tool. Most counseling that is done in church focuses on getting people saved, committed to Christ, or to trust God. These are important, but counseling must get to the deeper issues of the soul or a person might not be helped.

counselor can keep admonishing and the client can keep trying to overcome, but deliverance will not come forth or take many years or always be a struggle.

Second, you may not have the knowledge to find fulfillment. You resolve an issue by having the knowledge of God in your heart and applying this knowledge. This is something that has to be learned, whether through experience, the wisdom of others, revelation by the Spirit of God, or knowing the Word of God. It is not always finding and overcoming a sin that a problem is resolved. Instead, it might be identifying the driving force behind the sin and then dealing with that issue by the Word of God and the Spirit of God. This is the knowledge that is needed.

We must find fulfillment in order to have a victorious life. It has been said that all you need is God in order to be fulfilled, that God will fulfill you in every way and meet all your needs. This is true. God is everything for us, and when we have absolutely nothing, God is there for you to be in your heart and meet every need and give you the revelation you need. You can have absolutely nothing or be suffering terribly or be all alone, and you even can be in a bad situation because of your own fault and choices, but if you draw upon the Spirit of God, God will be your comfort, strength, love, and revelation. Moreover, the presence of God makes everything new and fresh. If you can receive the manifest presence of God, this is all you need to live another day.

However, God does not call us to sit in a cave or a closet all of our lives, unless, of course, He has called you to do this (and God does call some people to sit in a prison for a time). God has called us to worship and love Him, to love others, to build the kingdom of God, to become a better person and be conformed into the image of Christ. This is the will of God. If you are not fulfilling the will of God for your life, you will not find fulfillment. You are responsible for doing the will of God and fulfilling your destiny in God. People think that life is about fun and games, but life is about doing the will of God, and then you can have fun and games.

The search for fulfillment takes you on a journey that will help you fulfill the will God for your life and your destiny in God, and when you fulfill the will of God, you will find fulfillment. Before we take this journey to search for fulfillment, however, I must first share the personal pain that motivated me to write this book.

## My Journey in the Search for Fulfillment

About ten years ago during one Christmas season, when I was in a place where I had nothing in my life (except for God), I was crying out to God for more fulfillment. At the beginning of the new year, I earnestly sought God about this through prayer and meditation in the Word of God. In my heart I sensed God speaking to me that we find fulfillment through fulfilling work, meaningful relationships, and self improvement. About a month later I read the book, *The Purpose Driven Life* (by Rick Warren). This book confirmed to me what God had spoken to me, that we find fulfillment through work (ministry and missions), relationships (worship and fellowship), and self improvement (discipleship).

However, this low place in my life continued, and at the end of that year (on the first day of the new year) I had an emotional crisis. For the past four years there had been nothing in my life, and I also had come to the place where I was very discouraged about certain dreams and goals that had been unfulfilled for many more years than this. Finally, through certain circumstances and a deep hurt (which was the trigger), it got into my heart that I would never be successful and never have anything good in my life.

There had been low times before in my life, times that we all experience, when I would wrestle with discouragement and even depression, but I always had hope that life would improve, and so hopelessness and despair never took hold of me; they never gripped my heart. This time, however, hopelessness and despair totally and completely gripped my heart and overcame my soul (my mind, will, and emotions). I absolutely believed that I would never fulfill my dreams and never have anything good in life.

For the next five months I cried out to God at least once a day that there was no sense in living if this was going to be my life. I did not want to kill myself, but I did not see any purpose in living. There were times when I would cry, especially when I ate, because I did not see the sense of living anymore. For the first time I understood in my heart why some people try to kill themselves. The greatest pain in the world is to hate your life and sense a worthless existence with no real purpose and love and having absolutely no hope that the future will ever get better. I now knew this pain, and I understood for the first time how great this pain is and how it can drive you to do anything in order to stop the pain.

During this time I had some anxiety and depression issues. First, I did not have an appetite. I had to force myself to eat, and it literally would take me an hour just to eat a sandwich. I lost 15 pounds over this five month period, which was weight that I could not afford to lose, being a very slim person. I was surprised by this weight loss because it seemed that I was doing everything I could to try to eat, but I was rarely hungry and my stomach filled up fast.

I also had trouble sitting down or standing still, which was out of character for someone who loved to read and study and had made writing a hobby. I also could not concentrate, and therefore, during this time I could not write. I always had to be moving. If I could not sit, I had to pace back and forth. Even when I ate, I had to pace back and forth, and so during this time I could not have any sit down dinners and I could not eat with anybody. My work during this time was digging ditches and doing yard work, and although this menial labor was a factor that contributed to my feelings of hopelessness and despair, at least this was work I could do and not have to resign.

When I was home, I would get claustrophobic and could not stay inside for more than an hour. I had to go outside and walk. Even if it was pouring rain, I would go outside and walk, putting on short pants and sandals and carrying an umbrella. I dreaded it when it was lightning (which can be dangerous in Florida), for I had to get out and walk. I remember one night when it was raining and thundering and lightning very badly with flashes of white light all around, but I had to get out and walk. I prayed to God to protect me amidst the crashes of white light that exploded all around me. I was not harmed and I thank the Lord for His protection.

My practice was to walk until it was time to go to bed, which was about four hours of walking. When I was in bed, I could not lay on my back, for it caused feelings of terror. I always had to sleep on my stomach, and when I did this, I felt safer and calmer, but I still had feelings of anxiety and depression. And, of course, I had trouble sleeping. I had trouble falling asleep and I would wake up too early in the morning.

When I got up, I hoped the day would go by quickly. Every day this was my hope. The daily routine tasks of life, such as shaving, taking a shower, eating, and brushing my teeth became chores that I began to dread. It is difficult to explain why I dreaded these daily tasks, but I now believe that these daily tasks reminded me of the futility of my life, that I was doing the same old boring things every day and nothing was changing. I started shaving every other day and missing a shower one day a week in order to try to change my daily routine.[4]

I did not use any drugs, alcohol, tobacco, or medications during this time, but for the first time in my life I understood in my heart why people would do this to get through the day. You have to do what you have to do to maintain your sanity and responsibilities. There were times when I almost went to the doctor to try to get psychotropic or sleeping medication, but I never did.

How did I get through this crisis in one piece? First, I was able to identify that I was going down a dark and bad road and needed help. After about the first three weeks of this crisis, I saw myself going deeper into darkness in my soul, and I became very worried. I could see how my emotions were going down a path that I did not want to go down and that I could not seem to stop, even though I was born of the Spirit and filled with the Spirit. I was becoming almost terrified because I was afraid where this might lead. I could see my emotions being pulled to greater darkness, and I could see that I might wake up one day and truly want to kill myself or go crazy and be placed in a psyche ward.

I went to a minister who I respected and trusted and who had an anointing to break yokes. I told her what I was going through and asked her to pray for me. When she prayed for me, oppression lifted off of me, and from that day forward, my emotions stabilized. The hopelessness and despair still totally and completely gripped my heart, something I would have to battle for five months and that would only leave through working things out in my soul, but I had stopped going into deeper darkness. She prayed for me a second time about a month later, and I continued to remain emotionally stable. When you are in trouble, you have to ask God for help, and if you are in serious trouble, you also need the help of someone who knows God, and that someone should be

---

4- These experiences have helped me for working with troubled youth. Before, I would have seen certain behavior as being defiant or rebellious, but now I see it as maybe they are trying to cope with pain, anxiety, or hopelessness.

a person who has an anointing (a gift or an expertise) for that particular issue.

Second, deep down inside I still had hope in God, and it seemed like it was my spirit man and the Spirit of God speaking to my soul to have hope (Psalm 42:5,11). I had Jesus Christ in my heart and had faith in Him and believed that somehow God would help me and bring me out of this. This was strange, for the hopelessness and despair still totally and completely gripped my heart, but deep down inside, my spirit man and the Holy Spirit were speaking to me to have hope. I do not know what people do who are in a dark place and do not have God in their life. I am grateful to God for being my God and my being His child. Hope in God when you are in trouble, and have faith in His unfailing love.

Third, I sought God during this time with all of my heart, although strangely, I was not able to read the Bible for these five months. I knew the Bible better than most Christians, and even had a master's degree in theology, but I kept wondering how the Bible would help me through this crisis since I already knew what it said. I can see now that I was too sorrowful or bitter to read it, but I did end up reading and listening to the Scriptures.

During this time the only book I could read was a book by Pastor Jack Frost, *Experiencing the Father's Embrace* (and I also listened to his audio teachings).[5] This book had Scripture in it and had the verses I needed. This book had been in my heart to obtain, but I kept putting it off. I finally purchased a copy about two months before my crisis, but I did not read it until the crisis. It was a resource that I greatly needed and it always brought me great comfort. I did not realize that it would serve as my Bible for five months. You do need the word of God to help you through a crisis, but it may need to be a special word for your situation. I needed a greater revelation of the Father's love to get through this crisis.

Fourth, I made an extra effort to seek God for revelation about what to do and to obey His voice, with a willingness to do new things. Part of this revelation was making a special effort to be with people as much as possible, and I was soon attending four home fellowship groups each week. I also attended special prayer

---

5- I purchased a second copy and have loaned this book to some of the people I have counseled, and it has always been loved by those who read it.

meetings and services as much as I could. I also stepped out and did volunteer work that I never thought about doing before.

It is important that we hear God for revelation and are willing to do new things. This is an important way that God helps us. It has been said that if you want something new, you have to do something that you have never done before. You have to be willing to do new things if you want to see change.

I had seen many years ago how God helped the Israelites during the Exodus. The Lord did not destroy the Egyptian army at the beginning. Instead, He allowed them to chase the Israelites so that the people had to keep moving. God even told Moses to stop crying out to Him and to get up and get the people moving toward the Red Sea. God did this so that He could develop their faith and show them His glory in a greater way (Exod 14:1-18).

We may want God to give us immediate deliverance, but many times deliverance comes by walking things out in faith and doing new things and stepping out in faith and obeying what God is speaking to you. This is the word or voice you hear in your heart, which is the Spirit of God (the Holy Spirit) speaking to you.

Fifth, toward the end of this five months God gave me two things that I had asked Him for, although both times I had to step out in faith and do something. This answer to prayer gave me a lot of encouragement that God was with me and was helping me through this crisis. I still was not completely through the crisis, but the hopelessness and despair began to lift off of me. It is true what the Bible says,

"The Lord is close to the brokenhearted and saves those who are crushed in spirit" (Psalm 34:17, NIV; cf. Psalm 118:5, Isa 61:1).

About seven months later (at a Christmas party), still struggling but improving, I came across a woman who had just gotten her counseling degree at a Christian university. She told me about it, and it struck a chord with me. Even before my crisis I wanted training in counseling and began taking courses and reading books in this area, and I kept telling God that I wish I could be a counselor. I could teach, but I was not gifted in encouraging people and was never comfortable with counseling.

After my crisis, however, I now had the confidence that I could be a counselor. During my crisis I had entered a room that not too many people ever enter. I now knew in my heart the intense pain of total hopelessness and despair. I now knew in my heart why some people do not want to live. I now knew in my heart (not logical reasoning) why a person might try to kill him or herself. I now had understanding for these people, for I had been in that room of not seeing any purpose in living. I also knew in my heart that the next room, a room I never entered, was where people tried to kill themselves.

This confidence to counsel was now connected with a revelation that I had before my crisis. I had been ministering as a teacher, intercessor, and altar worker and had thought that this was all that was needed, but there came a time when I realized that many people needed more than this. They needed the ministry of counseling. I saw that there were certain life problems and issues of the soul that may never be completely resolved by just teaching and prayer, and while there is an anointing to deliver people from oppression, I also saw that if people did not change their thinking or did not resolve certain issues of the soul, they would go back into oppression and need deliverance again. I realized that there may have to be ministry where you take the time and sit down with a person (individually or in a care group) so that these issues of the soul and life problems can be completely brought to the light and dealt with by the Holy Spirit. I call this soul care ministry.[6] When I saw that so many people needed more than just teaching or prayer or deliverance, this is when I began to study counseling. I also began to tell God that I wish I could learn to be a counselor.

This wish to be a counselor started to become a reality. I applied to this counseling school, was accepted, and earned my master's degree in counseling. Since this time I have seen blessing and favour in my life. I had good success in one-on-one counseling at my internship. I also had success conducting a soul care group at

---

6- Soul care ministry is helping people deal with the deep issues of the soul and find inner healing and greater fulfillment. This is accomplished by letting people speak what is on their heart, helping them find strengths, assets, values, and desires, encouraging and speaking wisdom, helping them formulate the plans and initiate the actions that will give them a better life, and helping them trust God. This is done in the context of the Word of God and the Spirit of God.

my church. I was then a clinical therapist at a boys prison, and then I returned to Christian counseling. I now look back and see that this crisis experience was the only way I could have become a good counselor. I thank God for bringing me down this path. I am now happier and much more fulfilled than I was before. When you do the will of God, there is blessing and favour, and if you want to become gifted at something, you will have to go through some practical experience.

This book was inspired by my motivation to find greater fulfillment in life. The material within these pages has come from my training and education in counseling, my successful experiences in counseling and facilitating soul care groups, incorporating the teachings of gifted counselors and ministers,[7] revelation and insights from my own personal experiences and search for fulfillment, and the Word of God. The purpose of this book is to help you find greater fulfillment for your life, and it can also serve as a counseling and teaching tool.

You will find that finding fulfillment or success is never easy or quick, for finding fulfillment takes faith, commitment, character, good values, work, discipline, and perseverance. I have not reached total fulfillment in my life, for this is a journey rather than a destination, but I hope this book will guide you down the right path. I hope that these instructions will help you as much as they have helped me and those who I have counseled.

What has been written was written from my own particular perspective in life and is not meant to be an exhaustive examination for each subject, although much more could have been written. In fact, an entire book could have been written for each chapter (and this almost happened in the search for Freedom). I hope that this work will be a beginning and will provide a good foundation for finding greater fulfillment for your life

---

7- These counselors and ministers include Larry Crabb, Jack Frost (Shiloh Place), Robert McGee, Rick Warren, Gary Collins, Viktor Frankl, John Maxwell, Henry Cloud, John Townsend, Johnny Ray Lee (Turning Point).

## Chapter 2

# The Search for Meaning

We must find meaning in life in order to find fulfillment. Life must have meaning. This is a fundamental need that must be met. Even secular psychologists, although they may not be able to agree on how we find meaning, say that we are wired to find meaning in life. There is even a psychotherapy model (Logotherapy) which believes that the primary motivating force in human beings is to find meaning. We must find meaning in life if we hope to experience emotional wholeness and stability.

We live in an age, however, where people complain of feeling that their lives are totally and ultimately meaningless. When we become aware of the lack of meaning and fulfillment in our lives, it then becomes difficult to find joy in life. We might be haunted by feelings of emptiness and we might sense a void within. When these feelings continue for a long period of time, we can stop believing that life is meaningful.

This vacuum in the soul manifests itself in boredom, discontent, and loneliness, so that one battles anxiety and depression, hopelessness and fear. This frustration to find meaning may then be converted into a desire for power and position, a desire for money and possessions, or a desire for pleasure and love with maybe a focus on sexual gratification. All these pursuits are mere attempts to find meaning, to fill the void and emptiness. When there is void and emptiness in one's heart, there emerges a powerful drive to fill this hole and to find fulfillment.

The search for meaning is a search that is as old as time. People try to find meaning in work, activities, love, relationships, finding one's place in this world, learning new things, developing oneself as a person, having fun, or seeking the spiritual side of life. We want life to have value and to be enjoyable. We want to get out of bed with a sense of anticipation for the new day, having a heart that is full of peace, joy, love, faith, and hope and believing that life has meaning. We desperately want life to have meaning.

Meaning has been defined in various ways, and many times it is used interchangeably with purpose (being used as synonyms) and other times it is used in conjunction with purpose (with purpose being an aspect of meaning). Meaning and purpose are distinct ideas and will be treated as distinct ideas in this book, but they do come together and meet because it could be said that purpose is one aspect of meaning.

What is purpose? Purpose is what you do and is the how of life, asking, "How will I live (or what will I do)?" Purpose is setting before yourself an object (an object in view) that you hope to attain or accomplish. Thus, purpose is working and doing things, having relationships, and improving yourself and your life. These are the things that give you a reason for getting up in the morning.

Purpose can also ask the question, "Why am I here?" This is a relevant question for finding purpose, but it is also a question that is in the realm of meaning. This question is where purpose and meaning come together and meet, where purpose becomes an aspect of meaning, but meaning must go beyond purpose.

What is meaning? Meaning is what you believe and is the why of life, asking, "Why do I live?" Meaning determines your values and morals. Meaning is the intention and the significance of your existence. Meaning is what you are willing to die for. While both meaning and purpose will give you a reason for living, meaning also gives you a reason for dying. Your meaning for life should give you peace concerning death, and you should be willing to die for the beliefs that give you meaning. What are you willing to die for? Are you willing to die for your belief in God?

Meaning asks the existential questions (the questions of existence). We might ask the question- "What is the meaning of life?" or "What does it all mean?" However, when we ask what the meaning of life is, we are asking from a self centric perspective. This is not the best perspective, for it is God and life[1] who are

---

1- Why do I use life and God together? If you believe in God and follow what you believe is the will of God, you will try to do what God expects from you. However, if you do not know the will of God or what God expects from you in a certain situation, you can ask yourself what life expects from you, that is, what are your responsibilities in life and what is honorable toward others.

questioning us. It is not what we expect from life that is the central issue, a naïve desire of what we want to attain, create, and accomplish in life and what we think will give us meaning and fulfillment, but it is what God and life are expecting from us. God is questioning you about what is expected from you and what your responsibilities are in this life. God is asking you, "What meaning will you give to your life, and will your meaning in life be Me?" and "How will you be responsible with your life, and will you do My will?" Your answer to God is with the life you choose to live.

When we ask what the meaning of life is, the premise is that we want to know why we are here and what our destiny is. Even though we may have purpose in our relationships and what we do and reaching our full potential, we ultimately have questions about existence. Meaning tries to answer these eight questions: 1) Is there a God and what is God's nature? (divinity), 2) Where did I come from? (origin), 3) Who am I? (being), 4) Why am I here? (purpose), 5) Does my life have significance? (worth), 6) Why is there sin, wickedness, suffering, and death? (evil), 7) How should I live and why? (morality), 8) Where am I going? (destiny).

Meaning (and any worldview) must answer these questions, but most of all, meaning must embrace the reality of death and give an answer concerning our destiny. People do not like to talk about death, but death must be confronted if you want to discuss the meaning of life. Meaning must explain whether or not there is life after death, and if there is life after death, will this life after death be meaningful and better than this life, a life where we can truly experience peace, joy, goodness, and love.

This concept of life after death or eternity is the most important aspect of meaning and is really the key to finding meaning, because if this life is all there is and there is no eternity, then life really has no meaning. If death in this world is the end of self so that there is no conscious existence after death, then life in this world, if you are really honest, has no meaning.

This was the conclusion of the writer of the book of Ecclesiastes (which was probably King Solomon). He wrote about how he acquired power and money and possessions and how he gained great knowledge and wisdom about life and science and how he engaged in great projects of buildings and public works and agriculture and how he delighted in hobbies (like collecting

27

animals) and all the pleasures of life (having 1000 wives), but he concluded that it was all meaningless, and that life was especially meaningless for those who were oppressed and did not have a good life (Eccl 1:1-3:22, 1Kings 4:20-34, 9:10-10:29). He believed that life was meaningless because we all die in the end and he had no assurance in his heart of eternal life (Eccl 2:14-23, 3:18-22).

There are people who say that they do not care about life after death and are satisfied in just living an enjoyable life in this life and leaving a good foundation for their children and progeny, and with this they say that life has meaning for them. Whether these people are being honest and are really at peace with the thought of not having eternal life, for myself and others, this perspective is unacceptable. God has placed eternity in the heart of man (Eccl 3:11), and so there is no excuse for not seeing or desiring eternal life. We must believe that we have an immortal spirit and that there is life after death in order for life to have meaning, and if we embrace eternity and life after death, we must believe that there is a God who created us.

Life can only have meaning if there is a God who created us. This is a truth that has been stated by many religious leaders and philosophers. Even atheist existentialist philosophers, who believe that life has no meaning, have said that life can only have meaning if there is a God. Because they do not believe in God, however, they believe that life has no meaning other than the meaning that you give to it. They say that you must find your own meaning by finding your own reality. Thus, if there is no God and we are just matter so that this life is all there is and death is the end of self, then life has no meaning. Life then becomes just getting what you can get and having all the fun you can get and seeing eternity in your children and descendants. If you do not believe in life after death, then one's attitude will be- "Let us eat and drink and be merry, for tomorrow we may die" (1Cor 15:32b & Isa 22:13, Eccl 8:15 & Luke 12:19).

Atheists try to argue against the existence of God by saying that we make up God in order to find meaning in life, but if there is a God and this God created us in His image (Gen 1:26-27), then we will have a natural and instinctive desire to find meaning in life and to find God. This desire to know God is real because God is real and He created us. Those who believe in their heart that there is no God are fools (Psalm 14:1). There is a natural desire in us to find our Creator, to find God, and if we are not acting upon this innate desire, we are just denying or suppressing it.

How do we find meaning in life? The foundation for finding meaning is God. If there is a God who created us and who created us in His image with an immortal spirit, then life can only have meaning in God. Thus, we must find God in order to find meaning in life. Furthermore, the more we know God and experience Him, the greater meaning there will be in one's heart. God is the center and foundation of meaning.

## Section 2B: The 8 Questions of Meaning

If knowing God is how we find meaning in life, then we must know God. Ultimately, you must know God in your heart, but there is a revelation of the knowledge of God in the Scriptures. It is in the Scriptures where we can begin to find the answers to our questions about the meaning of life and how to know God. The Scriptures will be used as a basis for answering these eight questions of life. These eight questions are: divinity, origin, being, purpose, worth, evil, morality, and destiny.

I. There is the question of divinity: Is there a God and what is God's nature?

"The fool says in his heart, 'There is no God'" (Psalm 14:1a, NIV; cf. Psalm 49:1-20, 53:1-3).

"[1]The heavens declare the glory of God; the skies proclaim the work of his hands. [2]Day after day they pour forth speech; night after night they display knowledge" (Psalm 19:1-2, NIV; cf. Psalm 8:1-3, 26:7, 40:5, 111:4, Eccl 3:11, Heb 11:3, Rev 15:3).

"For since the creation of the world God's invisible qualities- his eternal power and divine nature- have been clearly seen, being understood from what has been made, so that men are without excuse" (Rom 1:20, NIV).

29

"Holy, holy, holy is the Lord God Almighty, who was, and is, and is to come" (Rev 4:8, NIV; cf. Rev 1:8, Isa 6:1-3).

Although the existence of God cannot be absolutely proven (but neither can God be disproved), the Scriptures say that it should be evident from at least nature that there is a Creator God. God has always been and is always present and will always be. The origin of God is truly a mystery that can never be known, at least in this life, but the presence of God should be evident by observing creation and seeing life and by sensing in one's heart or conscience that there is a God. There is a supernatural realm, and God lives in this realm. We have a supernatural spirit that was breathed into us by God, and this spirit within should tell you that there is a God and that this God is a distinct being that is separate from you and above you.

What is the nature of God? Whole books have been written on the nature of God and every systematic theology book contains at least one chapter describing God's nature. The description here, therefore, must be very brief, but there are some basic properties and qualities that can be highlighted.

First, God has a distinct identity. God is a living being and not a life force, being separate from Creation (Matt 22:31-32, 2Cor 6:16, Heb 12:27, Rev 7:2). God is a person who has a name and a personality (Exod 3:14- "I AM"). God is a spirit and lives in the supernatural realm, being invisible to the human eye (John 4:24).

Second, God is transcendent in that God transcends human life and the powerful forces of Creation. God is infinite and has no limits or bounds and transcends space (Job 11:7-9, 1Kings 8:27). God is eternal and everlasting so that God has no beginning or end and transcends time (Psalm 90:2, 102:25-27, Isa 57:15, John 8:58). God is unchanging in His character and qualities so that God transcends what has been created (Mal 3:6, Heb 13:8, James 1:17). If it ever appears that a quality or character trait of God has ended, it is because another one has taken over for addressing an issue.

Third, God has immutable and perfect character in Himself and His ways. God is holy (Isa 6:3, 43:3, 1Pet 1:16, Rev 15:4), which means that God is awesome and majestic and is perfect in purity, righteousness, integrity, goodness, and justice. God is love (Deut 7:6-8, Jer 31:3, Rom 5:8, 1John 4:8,16), which means that

God is self giving and is perfect in mercy (helping those in distress) and grace (giving ability and position without merit), exhibiting the qualities of forgiveness, compassion, patience, kindness, and goodness. God is truth (Psalm 141:6, Exod 34:6-7, Lam 3:21-23, John 16:13), which means that God is perfect and complete in knowledge, wisdom, integrity, and faithfulness. God will always be true to His covenants and promises.

Fourth, God embraces perfection and totality in what He is able to do. There are things that we can do, but we are limited in what we are able to do or we have to go one small step at a time. We are limited in power, knowledge, and presence, but God is not limited in these areas.

God is omnipotent (all powerful). This means that God is almighty in His works and power (Gen 18:14, 1Chr 29:11, Job 40:2, 42:2, Psalm 62:11, Jer 32:17, Luke 1:37, Eph 1:19-20, Heb 1:3). There is nothing that is too difficult for Him to accomplish or that is beyond His capabilities (although His power is always controlled by His character). This means that God can work miracles. Even though God has set forth powerful laws within matter and the heavenly bodies, God is not bound by Creation or natural laws. God is supernatural and is able to exert power to intervene in nature, and when He does intervene in nature, this is called a miracle.

God is omniscient (all knowing). This means that God knows all things and is all wise (Job 37:16, Psalm 147:5, Isa 40:14, 1John 3:20). There is nothing God does not know. God's mind encompasses all knowledge because He created all things. God beholds all things and is never deceived. God also knows the heart of a human being because He can read the spirit of a man or woman (1Chr 28:9, 1Sam 16:7, Psalm 119:68, 139:1-2). This makes God the perfect Judge. God also has perfect wisdom and is able to perfectly know what to do and how to do it (Psalm 104:24, Prov 3:19, 8:22-31, Dan 2:20-22, 1Cor 1:25, 2:7).

God is omnipresent (all present). This means that God is totally present everywhere in Creation (Isa 66:1, Jer 23:24, understanding that God is a distinct being and not part of Creation. God is also present for every human being (Psalm 139:7-12, Acts 17:27-28). This means that our whole life, our very existence, is in God. This presence of God is more intense and personal with the indwelling of the Holy Spirit through the reception of Jesus Christ into one's heart (Matt 28:20, John 14:17, 1Cor 6:19, 2Cor 1:22, Gal 4:6, Eph 2:22, 1John 4:13).

It must be concluded that God is glorious in every way. The glory of God, His radiant splendor and awesome majesty, shines forth in every aspect of His being and works.

But where is this glorious and almighty God? When Job was suffering, he cried out to God and asked where God was (Job 13:24, 14:13-17, 19:13-17, 23:1-17). When we are suffering, we want God to show up (Psalm 44:23-26). God does help us, but God is like the wind. We can sense His presence and see his workings, but we cannot see Him, for God is spirit (John 3:8, 4:24). It is interesting to note that both the Hebrew (*ruah*) and Greek (*pneuma*) word for spirit literally means "wind" or "breath". Furthermore, we do not know everything there is to know about God and it would be foolish and arrogant to think that we did. Therefore, we cannot judge what we want God to be or to do.

God told Moses that anyone who sees Him (the face of God) will die (Exod 33:12-23). Thus, we can only see a shadow of His glory. This may have a lot to do with the fact that we are made of flesh and are imperfect creatures (Isa 59:2). God even purposely hides Himself at times in order to force us to seek Him (Isa 45:15). God can baptize us with fire and the Holy Spirit and can refresh us with His Spirit and can anoint us with spiritual gifts, but you have to be hungry for God in order to experience these things. God shows Himself to those who hunger and thirst for Him and to those who are desperate for change or call out to Him.

God has made Himself known through His Son, Jesus Christ, who is the exact representation of God (Rom 1:4, 9:5, 2Cor 4:4, Phi 2:6, Col 1:15-20, 2:9, Heb 1:3, Rev 22:13). Jesus was made flesh and the Son of Man. He walked on the earth to testify about sin, righteousness, judgment, and God the Father. This testimony was written down by eye witnesses. The apostle John says,

"[1]In the beginning was the Word, and the Word was with God, and the Word was God. [2]He was with God in the beginning....[14]The Word became flesh and lived for awhile among us. We have seen his glory, the glory of the one and only Son, who came from the Father, full of grace and truth" (John 1:1-2,14, NIV, see 1:1-34; cf.

Prov 30:4, Matt 26:63-64, Mark 14:61-62, Luke 22:70, John 10:30,36-38, 12:45, 14:7-11).

"And I heard a loud voice from the throne saying, 'Now the dwelling of God is with men, and he will live with them. They will be his people, and God himself will be with them and be their God.'...³No longer will there be any curse. The throne of God and of the Lamb will be in the city, and his servants will serve him. ⁴They will see his face, and his name will be on their foreheads (Rev 21:4 and 22:3-4, NIV, see 21:1ff; cf. John 5:24-30).

There will come a time, after we have been glorified and there is made a new heaven and a new earth, when we will see Almighty God face to face. Until this time comes, however, God meets us Spirit to spirit. It is the depths of Him calling out to the depths of you, and the depths of you calling out to the depths of Him. Jesus said that we can only enter the kingdom of God by humbling ourselves as a little child (Matt 18:1-4, 19:13-15, Luke 18:15-17). Not seeing God face to face forces us to be humble as a little child. Moreover, if you were to see God face to face or see a spirit warning you to repent, you would still not be convinced if you did not believe the Scriptures (Luke 16:19-31), for believing in God requires giving your heart to Him. Giving your heart to God and becoming born again can only come forth by the Spirit of God connecting with your spirit through a humble heart.

There is one more question that must be asked when declaring the reality of God. This question is: How do I know God? Before this can be answered, however, certain truths must be established first. These truths will come forth from the answers to the other questions about existence, and the answer to the question of how we can know God will be given at the end of question eight.

II. There is the question of origin: Where did I come from?

"In the beginning God created the heavens and the earth....And the Lord God formed man from the dust of the ground and breathed into his nostrils the breath of life, and man became a living being" (Gen 1:1 and 2:7, NIV; cf. (Gen 2:22, Deut 32:6, Neh 9:6, Job 12:10, 33:4, Eccl 12:7, Heb 11:3).

"For you created my inmost being; you knit me together in my mother's womb" (Psalm 139:13, NIV, see 139:13-16).

"You are worthy, our Lord and God, to receive glory and honor and power, for you created all things, and by your will they were created and have their being" (Rev 4:11, NIV; cf. Acts 17:22-31, Rom 11:33-36, 1Cor 8:6).

We were created by God. God created all living things and breathed the breath of life into man and woman so that we have our life in God and have been created for God. Evolution did not create life and did not place us here on earth. The theory of evolution teaches that evolutionary forces are so powerful that it was slime plus time plus chance that produced life. Although evolutionists have shown that living organisms have a genetic ability to make changes for survival and adaptation (microevolution), there is no serious proof of any ability for a species to evolve into another species with different DNA (macroevolution). There is no such thing as going from a one celled organism to a lizard to a squirrel to a human being. The laws of nature are not sufficient and not powerful enough to go from species to species to species to form the human being.

There is also no such thing as theistic evolution, that a Creator created a one celled organism and then left it to evolve into a human being. This is similar in perspective to Deism. Deism believes in a God who created a clockwork universe, but then left us alone and does not want a relationship with us. It would be much easier for matter to evolve into a one celled organism than for a one celled organism to evolve into a human being. Therefore, theistic evolution soon gives way to atheistic evolution because the supposed evolutionary forces would be more powerful than a Creator God. If there is no need for a Creator God when going from a one celled organism to a human being, then there is no need for a Creator God when going from matter to a one celled organism.

If you had ten billion years with applied energy, you might have matter form into amino acids, but to form functional proteins by evolution is highly unlikely, and forming an RNA molecule is really too complex for evolution. Matter does not evolve into complex molecules, but tends toward disorder. Therefore, the theory of evolution violates the second law of thermodynamics (the law of entropy).

You can have all the billions of years you want, and at the most you might have a virus evolve (which is RNA wrapped in protein), but a virus is not life. The DNA molecule is extremely complex and so functionally specific so that it could never evolve from matter and proteins. The human DNA molecule is even more complex and functionally specific so that it would be impossible for it to evolve from a one celled organism. It is God who created our DNA, and from this DNA God created man and woman. Evolution is merely a theory for those who do not want to believe in a God or in a God who will hold us accountable for our lives. Our origin is God Almighty who created all matter and energy and who formed the universe and all life by His direct hand.[2]

III. There is the question of being: Who am I?

"So God created man in his own image, in the image of God he created him; male and female he created them" (Gen 1:27, NIV; Note: It requires male and female together to comprise "man" (*adam*) and "the image of God"; cf. Gen 1:26, 5:1-2, 9:6, Psalm 8:5 & Heb 2:7, James 3:9).

"Yet You have made him [man] a little lower than God, and You crown him with glory and majesty!" (Psalm 8:5, NASB; cf. Matt 6:26, Acts 17:25-29).

---

2- I comment on this subject from my own studies on the theory of evolution and my expertise in science (having a B.S. degree in chemistry with some graduate work in biochemistry and a specialty in DNA and genetics). This includes writing two college term papers on the subject of evolution and reading *On the Origin of Species* by Darwin. It is interesting to note that Darwin's grandfather also published a book on evolution, so evolution was in his bloodline. While Darwin's own book on evolution supplied wonderful evidence for microevolution and did an outstanding analysis of this subject, he gave no real evidence for macroevolution. His conclusion was that the evolutionary forces are so powerful that there has to be evolution from one species to another. He believed that evidence for this would be found in the future, but no real evidence or solid proof for this has come forth.

"I praise you because I am fearfully and wonderfully made; your works are wonderful, I know that full well" (Psalm 139:14, NIV; see 139:13-16).

You were created in the image of God. What does it mean to be created in the image of God? God created us to be like Him and He breathed into us the breath of life, imparting into us an immortal spirit. This means that the human spirit never dies. This means that we have intelligence and can understand Creation, being able to study matter, life, and scientific laws and understand these things. This means that we can develop language and writing and speak clearly with many sounds. This means that we can think spiritual and philosophical thoughts and that there is a desire in our hearts to be connected to our Creator. This means that we are able to love and to be loved and to have relationships and that we have emotions and feelings and can appreciate beauty. This means that we can create, invent, investigate, and discover. This means that we have a moral conscience. This means that we have a free will.

However, we also have another side, a dark side, which has corrupted this image of God. Man and woman rebelled against God, and it was really in search of becoming one's own god that man and woman disobeyed God and became sinners (Gen 3:1-24). The root of sin is to want to be your own god. We are now born into sin through Adam and we choose to sin.

"9The heart is deceitful above all things and beyond cure. Who can understand it? 10'I the Lord search the heart and examine the mind, to reward a man according to his conduct, according to what his deeds deserve'" (Jer 17:9-10, NIV, see 17:5-10).

"There is no difference, 23for all have sinned and fall short of the glory of God" (Rom 3:22b-23, NIV).

Christianity is the only religious system that emphasizes the fallen nature of man and woman. This might sound negative, but it is not about being positive or negative, it is about truth, it is about reality, and this reality is clearly set forth in the Scriptures and should be evident in your heart. The solution for sin will be given in question six (VI).

IV. There is the question of purpose: Why am I here?

"[13]Now all has been heard; here is the conclusion of the matter: Fear God and keep his commandments, for this is the whole duty of man. [14]For God will bring every deed into judgment, including every hidden thing, whether it is good or evil" (Eccl 12:13-14, NIV).

"Jesus replied, 'Love the Lord your God with all your heart and with all your soul and will all you mind.' This is the first and greatest commandment. And the second is like it: 'Love your neighbor as yourself'" (Matt 22:37-39, NIV; cf. Deut 6:4-5, Mark 12:29-31).

"Do unto others as you would have them do unto you" (Luke 6:31, NKJV, see Matt 7:12a).

"Then I heard every creature in heaven and on earth and under the earth and on the sea, and all that is in them, singing: To him who sits on the throne and to the Lamb be praise and honor and glory and power, for ever and ever!" (Rev 5:13, NIV; cf. Psalm 67:1-7, 150:1-6, Isa 42:10-12).

God created us in love as a Father and for relationship with Him and others. Thus, we must live our lives for God, the One who created us. We must worship our Creator and glorify His name. This is the purpose of our existence. If we try to lift ourselves up, to be our own god, we will only get into sin. We are to love God and others and obey His commandments while we live on this earth. Even after the writer of Ecclesiastes declares that life is meaningless, he concludes that the one purpose we have in life is to obey God's commands and do what is good.

God lives in another realm and another dimension, but there will be a day when God will live with us face to face. There is this present age and the age to come, but in both ages we are to obey God's commands and do what is good, which is loving God and others and giving God the glory. This is our eternal purpose.

V. There is the question of worth: Does my life have significance?

"Then God said, 'Let us make man in our image, in our likeness, and let them rule over the fish of the sea and the birds of the air, over the livestock, over all the earth, and over all the creatures that move along the ground.'...God blessed them and said to them, 'Be fruitful and increase in number; fill the earth and subdue it. Rule over the fish of the sea and the birds of the air and over every living creature that moves on the ground'" (Gen 1:26,28, NIV).

"You made him [man] ruler over the works of your hands; you put everything under his feet" (Psalm 8:6, NIV).

"[5]Your love, O Lord, reaches to the heavens, your faithfulness to the skies. [6]Your righteousness is like the mighty mountains, your justice like the great deep. O Lord, you preserve both man and beast. [7]How priceless is your unfailing love! Both high and low among men find refuge in the shadow of your wings" (Psalm 36:5-7, NIV).

We are created in the image of God and God has given us dominion and stewardship over the earth with the ability to learn the secrets of life and the universe. We also were created in love by a Father who wanted children. Thus, there is much significance in one's life. No matter how you see yourself, God thinks a lot about you, for you were created in love and for love by God to have relationship with Him and others and to enjoy and have dominion over the world He has created.

You have much worth in God's eyes as one who is created in the image of God. God also sees you as a unique individual, and you have gifts and abilities that will enable you to have dominion over the earth. Each person has a unique DNA pattern and a unique spirit so that no two people are alike. This means that each person has a uniqueness to be offered to this world and for building the kingdom of God, and, moreover, each person can have a unique relationship with God. You are a unique individual and have a significant place in this world to do the will of God and help build the kingdom of God.

"'For I know the plans I have for you,' declares the Lord, 'plans to prosper you and not to harm you, plans to give you hope and a future'" (Jer 29:11, NIV).

God always has good plans for your life and is always working for your good (Rom 8:28). You just have to follow Him, and even when you fail or tribulation comes against you, do not quit and continue following Him.

Finally, even when you do not care about God or do not want God, God still pursues you as a lover pursues a beloved or as a Father pursues a wayward child, and even when you are not able to sense God, God sees you and reaches down to you and calls you to Him (Hos 1:10, 2:23, Isa 55:1-2, 57:15, 65:1, Rev 22:17). You are worth so much to God that He even sent His only Son to die on a cross for your sins. This truly makes your life significant.

VI. There is the question of evil: Why is there sin, wickedness, suffering and death in this world (especially if there is supposed to be an all good and all powerful God)?

"He [Jesus] replied, 'I saw Satan fall like lightening from heaven'" (Luke 10:18, NIV; cf. Job 1:6-7, 2:1-2, Isa 14:11-15, Ezek 28:14-17, Zech 3:1, John 8:44, Rev 12:7-17).

"22And the Lord God said, 'The man has now become like one of us, knowing good and evil. He must not be allowed to reach out his hand and take also from the tree of life and eat, and live forever.' 23So the Lord God banished him from the Garden of Eden to work the ground from which he had been taken. 24After he drove the man out, he placed in front of the Garden of Eden cherubim and a flaming sword flashing back and forth to guard the way to the tree of life" (Gen 3:22-24, NIV; see 3:1-24; cf. Psalm 51:5, 53:3).

"Therefore, just as sin entered the world through one man, and death through sin, and in this way death came to all men, because all sinned....for all have sinned and fall short of the glory of God" (Rom 5:12 & 3:23, NIV; cf. Rom 6:23, 7:14, Gen 3:1-24, Psalm 51:5, 53:3).

"We all, like sheep, have gone astray, each of us has turned to his own way; and the Lord has laid on him [the Messiah] the iniquity of us all" (Isa 53:6, NIV, see 52:13-53:12).

"[8]Again, the devil took him [Jesus] to a very high mountain and showed him all the kingdoms of the world and their splendor. [9]'All this I will give you,' he said, 'if you will bow down and worship me.' [10]Jesus said to him, 'Away from me, Satan! For it is written: 'Worship the Lord your God, and serve him only'" (Matt 4:8-10, NIV).

How does one reconcile evil and suffering with the concept of a Creator God who is all good and all powerful? Where is this God in the midst of all this evil and suffering, and why is there death? Any worldview must address the issue of evil and suffering and offer an answer for this.

The issue of evil and suffering is why so many people decide to not believe in a God, but this is bitterness and a refusal to see the truth. When we complain about evil, we are saying that there is good and there are moral absolutes, and if there is good and there are moral absolutes, then there must be a God who created us and imparted into us a spirit that is in His image and has a moral conscience. If you complain about evil, then you are implying that there is a God.

Other people do not want to worship a God who would allow evil, suffering, and death, but, again, this comes out of bitterness and a refusal to see the truth. The answer to the issue of evil, suffering, and death is found by looking within, not by looking outward and demanding that God do something about all this bad stuff. We must get a revelation of how evil, suffering, and death entered this world and what God has decided to do about it.

We and the heavenly beings (the angels) were all created in perfection, but everyone was also given a free will, having been created in the image of God. When the archangel Lucifer (Satan) became proud and tried to lift himself up to be worshipped (Isa 14:9-17, Ezek 28:11-19), he and the angels who followed him were cast out of heaven by God. However, God did not chain Satan but allowed him to test man and woman, who had been given dominion over the earth.

When man and woman were enticed by Satan and wanted to be gods and disobeyed God, there was irreparable damage to the human soul and life radically changed for humanity and the earth. Corruption entered into the spirit and body of man and woman, resulting in immediate spiritual death (being separated from God) and later physical death (with sickness and disease). Corruption also entered into the earth and all life on it. Moreover, man and woman lost dominion over the earth and Satan became the ruler of the earth, with man and woman in bondage to sin and the kingdom of darkness. Evil now reigns over the earth with man and woman sinners. Thus, God allows evil, suffering, and death because these are the consequences of rebelling against God and believing Satan.

Satan is called the "ruler (*arche*)" of the earth and "the god of this age" (Luke 4:5-8, 22:53, John 12:31, 14:30, 16:11, Acts 26:18, 1Cor 2:8, 8:5-6, 10:20, 2Cor 4:4, Gal 1:4, 4:8, Eph 2:1-2, 6:10-12, Heb 2:14-15, 1John 5:19). This means that he has dominion over the earth (just as man and woman had dominion) and that he is the spirit (the god) who reigns over those who are not submitted to the Lord God Almighty. This is all the result of the transfer of power from man and woman to Satan (Gen 3:1-24). Humans still have a free will and can be in conflict and not in alignment with the spirits of darkness, but if one is not aligned with God, you will always be deceived and defeated by the forces of darkness.

Thus, concerning evil and suffering, it can be said that God's hands are tied to a certain degree, although He is still God and Ruler over all the earth (Psalm 24:1). The Lord God Almighty is still Lord over all and has the ultimate power and authority over Satan and the kingdom of darkness, just as the Lord had ultimate power and authority over man and woman when they were given dominion over the earth, but Satan somehow earned a certain type of legal right over the earth as well as all human beings who are not submitted to the Lord God Yahweh (the Great I AM). Furthermore, there is also the issue of sin. We are sinners who create our own suffering through the sin and evil we engage in, and God cannot change our fallen natures without some type of restitution or repentance on our part, for we are spiritually dead and our spirits are corrupted beyond human repair.

What is the answer? It is only through redemption in Jesus Christ that one is reconciled to God and one's spirit is regenerated and bondage to Satan is broken. God has made a way for us in the midst of this dilemma by sending His Son to die on a cross for our sins and to free us from the power of Satan and to give us power and authority over Satan and the kingdom of darkness. God has decided to use our fallen state for His glory, to show forth His grace and mercy for all the created beings to see (Rom 11:32-36).

"For God so loved the world that he gave his one and only Son, that whoever believes in him shall not perish but have eternal life" (John 3:16, NIV, see 3:1-21).

"But God demonstrates his own love for us in this: While we were still sinners, Christ died for us....For the wages of sin is death, but the gift of God is eternal life in Christ Jesus our Lord" (Rom 5:8 & 6:23, NIV; cf. Rom 10:9-10).

"[13]For he has rescued us from the dominion of darkness and brought us into the kingdom of the Son he loves, [14]in whom we have redemption, the forgiveness of sins" (Col 1:13-14, NIV; cf. Rom 3:24, 8:23, Gal 3:13-14, Eph 1:7,14, 4:30, Heb 9:12, 1Pet 1:18-21).

"[4]But when the time had fully come, God sent his Son, born of a woman, born under law, [5]to redeem those under law, that we might receive the full rights of sons. [6]Because you are sons, God sent the Spirit of his Son into our hearts, the Spirit who calls out, 'Abba, Father'. [7]So you are no longer a slave, but a son; and since you are a son, God has made you also an heir" (Gal 4:4-7, NIV, *see Gal 3:26-29*; cf. John 1:13, 3:3-8, Rom 8:14-17, 8:29-39, 9:25-26, 1Cor 6:19-20, 2Cor 1:21-22, 3:18, 4:16, 5:5,17, 6:16, Eph 1:3-10, 1:13-14, 4:24, Col 3:10, 1Tim 1:14, Titus 3:3-7, 1Pet 1:3,23, James 1:18, 1John 3:24, 4:13).

It was in love that God created us, and it is in love that He offers us forgiveness and a way out of our sin so that we can be redeemed and rescued from the kingdom of darkness. And not only are we redeemed and rescued from the kingdom of darkness through faith in Jesus Christ, but we are born again, born of the Spirit. This means that your spirit is regenerated into the image of

God and you become a true child of God. Thus, God has seen our situation and has reached down to us and has called us to Him through the cross of Jesus Christ, but you must reach out to God.

"[9]That if you confess with your mouth the Lord Jesus and believe in your heart that God has raised Him from the dead, you will be saved. [10]For with the heart one believes to righteousness, and with the mouth confession is made to salvation" (Rom 10:9-10, NKJV; see 10:9-13; cf. John 3:16-21,36, Acts 2:27, 4:12, Eph 1:7, Phi 2:10-11, Rev 3:20, 21:17).

If you confess that you are a sinner and believe in Jesus Christ as your Savior and confess Him as your Lord, you will receive forgiveness of your sins and become born of the Spirit and enter into the kingdom of God and eternal life. When you pass from this present age, you will enter into life in heaven with God and be resurrected at the last day (which is the redemption of your body).

This present age must reach its completion before our redemption can be made complete (Matt 13:24-50, 24:1-31, Luke 21:28, Rom 8:18-25, Eph 4:30, 2Thes, 2:1-12, 2Pet 3:3-13). This will come about when Jesus Christ returns a second time to set up the eternal kingdom of God upon the earth. During this present age God sows good seed to make sons of God and Satan sows bad seed to make sons of darkness (Matt 13:24-30 and 13:36-43).

The presence of evil, suffering, and death, therefore, should cause us to seek God. God uses suffering for His will and purposes, using it as a tool for forming good character in us (Rom 5:3-5) and helping us seek God and His righteousness. Suffering is a separating tool that causes people to either seek God or reject God, to either seek the light or stay in the darkness. If life was too much fun and full of enjoyment but we were still sinners, we would not see our need for God. Suffering is the tool that can lead you to God and His righteousness if you are willing to see the darkness within you and your need for the grace of God.

There is one final question on this subject. What should we do about suffering and evil? First, persevering in righteousness through suffering is what forms good character in us (Rom 5:3-5). This is why we are exhorted to endure suffering as discipline from God (Heb 12:5-13). Second, suffering and evil should cause us to

43

seek God and draw close to God and make Him our Rock and Fortress. Third, it is our responsibility to help one another through the suffering of this world and to protect each other from evil. You are your brother's keeper.

VII. There is the question of morality: How should I live and why?

"The fear of the Lord is the beginning of wisdom, and knowledge of the Holy One is understanding" (Prov 9:10, NIV; cf. Job 28:28, Psalm 12:8, 19:9, 111:10, 112:1, Prov 16:6, 28:26, Isa 11:1-3, Luke 18:2, 2Cor 5:11).

"5Know then in your heart that as a man disciplines his son, so the Lord your God disciplines you. 6Observe the commands of the Lord your God, walking in his ways and revering him" (Deut 8:5-6, NIV, see 8:1-20; cf. Prov 3:11-12, Heb 12:5-13).

"Jesus answered, 'It is written: Man does not live on bread alone, but on every word that comes from the mouth of God'" (Matt 4:4, NIV; cf. Deut 8:3b).

"6God will give to each person according to what he has done. 7To those who by persistence in doing good seek glory, honor and immortality, he will give eternal life. 8But for those who are self seeking and who reject the truth and follow evil, there will be wrath and anger....So then, each of us will give an account of himself to God" (Rom 2:6-8 & 14:12, NIV, see 2:6-16; cf. Psalm 62:12, Matt 7:24, 12:50, Luke 6:46-49, John 7:17, 8:31-32, 14:15,21,23-24, 15:10,12,14, James 1:25, 1John 5:3, 2John 1:6, Rev 20:11-15).

The Lord God Almighty is righteousness and He is the Law giver. If we are created by God in His image, then morality must come from God and a basic understanding of this morality will be in our conscience. If there is a God who created us and this God has given us laws to live by, then we must follow these laws to the best of our ability and stay away from wickedness and an evil heart. This is the fear of the Lord. The reason why a lot of people do not want to believe in God is because they do not want to be accountable to anyone or any moral law, but there will be a day of judgment when God judges each person according to one's deeds.

How do we live a moral life and abide by certain standards? The primary motivation for living a moral life is to live for the sake of someone or something. You must be committed to a cause, an organization, a family, a loved one, or God. If you are committed to serving and following God, then you will be motivated to follow the commands of God. There is a secondary motivation for living a moral life. It is the fear of getting into trouble or being embarrassed. This is a good motivator, especially since we are sinners, but if you do not have the primary motivation of a commitment (especially a commitment to God), then your moral habits will be inconsistent and even poor. There must be a positive focus of serving and following God if you hope to live a moral life. Ultimately, in order to truly obey God, you have to be committed to Jesus Christ as your Savior and Lord.

There are strong and loud voices today that man is just a product of heredity and environment and does not have a moral conscience and is not responsible for his actions. This theory believes that we are nothing more than the result of biological, psychological, and sociological conditions and forces, a view that has been fostered and strengthened by psychoanalytical theory (primarily with Freud). This view reduces man into a body of matter with no spirit and makes him into a robot, not a human being, so that it is thought that man is not self determining.

It is true that we are finite and imperfect creatures and that heredity and environment can place restrictions upon us, but we do have a free will and have the ability to make choices. It is also true that it might be easy to initially make wrong choices and go down the wrong path, but we have the ability to see that we are on the wrong path and to change. It is also true that we are sinners, but we can still make changes, for the human spirit has some ability to break free from certain things. Even if there is something that we are in bondage to and cannot get free of, we can still choose to call out to God and others for help. God expects even the most depraved sinner to be convicted of his sins and to call out to Him and receive Jesus Christ as his Savior and Lord. God has set a day of judgment and will hold us accountable for our behavior. Thus, we are definitely self determining creatures with a free will.

Viktor Frankl (founder of Logotherapy) strongly believes that we are self determining creatures. He was interned in Nazi concentration camps for three years during World War II, being imprisoned because he was Jewish. He was already a psychotherapist before he was imprisoned (a psychiatrist with a medical degree), and he was even a colleague of Freud. He called the concentration camps a "living laboratory" and a "testing ground" for human behavior. For him these camps proved that we are self determining and can choose how we will behave (if we are not afraid to die). He said that some men in the concentration camps acted like "swine" (including inmates) while others acted like "saints" (including prison guards). He concluded by saying, "Man has both potentialities within himself; which one is actualized depends on decisions but not on conditions."[3]

Thus, even though we are sinners who are in bondage to sin and the kingdom of darkness, we still have a free will and a conscience. This conscience resides in the spirit, which is the image of God within us (although corrupted without Christ). This is where God speaks to us. The greatest proof that we have a free will and are self determining creatures is that God holds us accountable for our actions and will judge us accordingly. While we can never be reconciled to God or truly obedient to God if we are not in Christ, having a free will and being a self determining creature means that, even if we are not in Christ, God expects us to follow our conscience and to see that one is a sinner who is in need of the grace of God.

VIII. There is the question of destiny: Where am I going?

"[30]At that time the sign of the Son of Man will appear in the sky, and all the nations of the earth will mourn. They will see the Son of Man coming on the clouds of the sky, with power and great glory. [31]And he will send his angels with a loud trumpet call, and they will gather his elect from the four winds, from one end of the heavens to the other" (Matt 24:30-31, NIV; Note: "Son of Man" is a messianic title that comes from Daniel 7:13-14.).

---

3- Viktor Frankl, *Man's Search for Meaning*, trans. by Ibse Lasch (Boston: Beacon Press, rev., 1962), p. 136.

"[40]As the weeds are pulled up and burned in the fire, so it will be at the end of the age. [41]The Son of Man will send out his angels, and they will weed out of his kingdom everything that causes sin and all who do evil. [42]They will throw them into the fiery furnace, where there will be weeping and gnashing of teeth. [43]Then the righteous will shine like the sun in the kingdom of their Father. He who has ears, let him hear" (Matt 13:40-43, NIV; see 13:24-30 and 13:36-43; cf. Matt 13:44-52).

"And I heard a loud voice from the throne saying, "Now the dwelling of God is with men, and he will live with them. They will be his people, and God himself will be with them and be their God....He who overcomes will inherit all this, and I will be his God and he will be my son" (Rev 21:3 & 21:7, NIV; cf. Rom 9:25-26, Gal 3:26-29, Rev 5:7-10).

There are two destinies offered to us. You can remain in your sin and reject the cross of Jesus Christ and continue down the road of destruction that will terminate in eternal death, or you can accept Jesus Christ as Savior and Lord and receive entrance into the kingdom of God and eternal life. This is your choice. What will you do with the cross? This is the question that God is asking you.[4]

The question of destiny leads us back to the issue of death, and we must ask the question: Is there life after death and what kind of life will this be? The writings of the Old Testament are vague in their understanding of life after death. There was more of a hope in a life after death than an absolute belief in it. The writer of Ecclesiastes said that life is meaningless because he had no absolute assurance of life after death. Life truly is meaningless if this life is all there is and death means the end of self. How can you live if you believe that death is the end of self? This thought should drive anyone who is willing to contemplate the issue of death to a crisis of conscience.

---

4- For those who do not hear the gospel of Jesus Christ but know they are sinners and try to live by God's laws (Rom 1:18-20, 2:13-16,25-29), this is for God to judge what He will do, but they still must receive Christ. For those who hear the gospel of Jesus Christ but reject it till their dying day, they have cut themselves off from God's grace. When you are confronted with the cross of Jesus Christ, you have to make a decision.

The revelation of Jesus Christ offers us clear evidence of life after death. Jesus Christ was put to death on a cross, buried in a tomb, and then rose from the dead by the power of God, giving proof that He was the Son of God and the Jewish Messiah. It also gave proof that He destroyed the power of death and holds the keys to death and hell and that eternal life comes only by the grace of God and faith in Him. Jesus said,

"I am the resurrection and the life. He who believes in me will live, even though he dies; and whoever lives and believes in me will never die" (John 11:25-26, NIV; cf. John 3:16, 5:24-30, 1Cor 15:3-4,12-26,54-57, 1Thes 4:14-16, Heb 2:14-15, 1John 3:8, Rev 1:18; Isa 25:8, Hos 13:14).

"This grace was given us in Christ Jesus before the beginning of time, [10]but it has now been revealed through the appearing of our Savior, Christ Jesus, who has destroyed death and has brought life and immortality to light through the gospel" (2Tim 1:9b-10, NIV; cf. Matt 26:27-28, 28:5-7, Acts 2:22-33, 3:14-15, 4:33, 10:39-41, 17:2-3, Rom 1:4, 4:25-5:1, 5:12-17, 10:9, Eph 1:19b-20, Heb 2:14-15, 1Pet 1:3, 3:18, Rev 1:18, 2:11, 5:1-14, 21:4).

You must come to the cross. The cross signifies both life and death for us. The cross says that we are sinners who deserve eternal death. This is the offense of the cross. The cross also offers us eternal life in the kingdom of God. This is the wonder and the miracle of the cross. Jesus said,

"For God so loved the world that he gave his one and only Son, that whoever believes in him shall not perish but have eternal life" (John 3:16, NIV; cf. Rom 10:9-10).

"[31]Now is the time for judgment on this world; now the prince of this world will be driven out. [32]But I, when I am lifted up from the earth, will draw all men to myself" (John 12:31-32, NIV, see 12:23-36; cf. John 8:28, 19:16-18, Matt 20:17-19; Note: The term "lifted up" is a metaphor for being crucified; see John 3:14-15 for "the bronze snake" in Numbers 21:4-9).

"I am the way and the truth and the life. No one comes to the Father except through me" (John 14:6, NIV).

Coming to the cross is the beginning of finding meaning in life. When you believe in Jesus Christ, receiving Him into your heart as Savior and Lord, you will know God, and as you follow Christ, you will be on the path to knowing God more and finding greater meaning in life.

## Section 2C: Finding Meaning

How do we find meaning in life (understanding that it is God who is asking us how we will find meaning in life and will we find meaning in Him)? First, meaning is found by knowing why you are here on earth and where you are going. You are created by God in the image of God and can have eternal life in the kingdom of God through Jesus Christ, the Son of God. This means that your life has much significance and worth

Second, counselors and psychologists say you will find meaning in life by living for something (a cause) that is greater than you and living for someone who is greater than you or dear to you (and this can be a people group). You will also find meaning by feeling socially connected to your world. Christian counselors say you will find meaning in life by living for God and giving yourself to the cause of the gospel of Jesus Christ, which includes loving God and others and being connected to a body of believers. This is all true. Let us go over in more detail these three concepts.

You find meaning by giving yourself to a cause that is greater than you, especially for helping people. This principle is affirmed by leaders in every profession, especially in the realm of politics. I have read books and articles from those who have served in government, and a common theme is how politics has given that person meaning and purpose in life because it was working for a great cause that helped people. Although politics can be more self serving than serving and many times what is thought to help people does not help, it is true that giving yourself to a cause that is greater than yourself and helps people will provide a great sense of meaning and purpose for your life.

You find meaning by making a commitment to a person or a people who you will live your life for, with this person or people considered to be greater than you or dear to you. You can live your life for a loved one, your family, your friends, your community, your nation, the world, or God. A person serving in government might give his or her life to the community, state, or nation that he or she is serving. If you live your life for God, this is with the view of helping others, for the second greatest commandment is to love your neighbor as yourself.

This is how you will find meaning in life. You will find meaning in life by living for a cause that is greater than yourself. Will this cause be the cross and the gospel of Jesus Christ? You will find meaning in life by living for someone who is greater than you or dear to you. Will this someone be God the Father and His Son Christ Jesus? When you live your life for God, you will have lasting purpose because God is always with you and His kingdom is the only lasting kingdom.

You will also find meaning in life by being connected to others. Will you make an effort to develop your relationship with God and the family of God and to love your neighbor? When you are living for God and giving yourself to the cause of the gospel of Jesus Christ and feel connected to God and the family of God and your neighbor, your life will have meaning and you will have hope of the future.

If I was asked what Scripture passage is the meaning of life, I would cite what Jesus said in Matthew 22:37-39 (quoted earlier). These are the two greatest commandments and confirm what was said above. These commandments instruct you to love God with all of your heart, mind, soul, and strength and to love your neighbor as yourself. We love God by doing His will and worshiping Him. We love others by helping them and building them up and being good to them. You love yourself by reaching your full potential and creativity and becoming who God created you to be. Some will say that meaning comes by glorifying God, but glorifying God is to love God and others. These two commandments are the biblical foundation for finding meaning in life.

Finally, it should be evident that we can find meaning in life in more than one way and in different things, but let the center and foundation for your meaning in life be God.

How might we discover greater meaning for our lives, especially at those times when we seem to be stuck in life and need change? Viktor Frankl believes that we can discover meaning in three different ways.[5] First, we can discover meaning by doing a deed (especially a selfless deed). This is when we do something to help others or accomplish something that requires effort and faith. If you want change in your life, you might have to step out in faith and do something that you have never done before.

Second, we can discover meaning by experiencing a value (especially love), and this can be through another person or an action you perform or personal meditation (which can include nature and art). This is when you experience or receive a value from someone (e.g., you are loved by someone) or when you develop a value from an action or work that you perform or when you receive a revelation of a value.

Third, we can discover meaning through suffering, with suffering having the highest potential for leading us to greater meaning. Suffering is defined as having any kind of distress, misery, or pain. If you are going through torment or affliction or a battle or a storm or you are experiencing any kind of a trauma, hurt, obstacle, or hardship, this is suffering.

These are excellent ways for exploring and discovering greater meaning for one's life. The first two are simple concepts to understand, but the third one is difficult to see. How does one find meaning through suffering? This may sound strange to those who live in the modern society, but this is really a biblical principle (Matt 5:10-12, Luke 6:20-23, Phi 3:7-14). Frankl sets forth the basic premise for why we can and must find meaning through suffering. When he was in the death camps, he asked himself, "Has all this suffering, this dying around us, a meaning? For, if not, then ultimately there is no meaning to survival; for a life whose meaning depends upon such a happenstance- as whether one escapes or not- ultimately would not be worth living at all."[6]

If you cannot find meaning when you are suffering, then life really has no meaning, for this means that you must have happy circumstances and be achieving things in order to find fulfillment,

---

5- Frankl, *Man's Search for Meaning*, p. 113.
6- Frankl, *Man's Search for Meaning*, p. 117.

but meaning must be greater than this. Meaning must be greater than accomplishing and attaining things. Meaning must be greater than enjoyment, having fun, or being happy. You have to have a why to live, not a how, in order to find meaning in life. Meaning is the why of life. We might know how to live and what gives us purpose and enjoyment, but if we do not know why we are living, if we ever come to a place where we no longer enjoy life or have purpose, life will no longer have meaning for us. This is why suffering is the true test for finding meaning. If you cannot find meaning through suffering, then your life is not rooted and grounded in what is meaningful.

When life has no more meaning for us, we may not care about living anymore and even not care about living forever. This might be why some people seem to not care about life after death. If life is no longer enjoyable and you no longer have purpose, then there is no reason to continue living, and why should you think that any life after death would be better. When meaning can only be gained through achievement and enjoyment, then it is easy to become disappointed about life and to even lose courage for living. If these feelings continue, you will be overcome with depression, and if depression continues, you will be overcome with hopelessness and despair. When this happens, you lose hope of the future, believing that you will never find happiness or, if you have found some measure of happiness, you no longer enjoy life and happiness has become a decreasing commodity. You must find meaning in more than what brings you enjoyment, achievement, or happiness.

If you ever come to the place where you have no ability for outer achievement or enjoyment, except to survive, there can still be an inner achievement and joy by suffering with dignity and integrity. Suffering with dignity and integrity is holding on to your values and beliefs (whatever you believe is important) and being willing to die for the cause and the person you are living for.

If you are living for Jesus Christ and the gospel, it is being true to Christ and the gospel through your suffering. It is serving God and doing the will of God and loving others in the midst of one's suffering. It is living in joy, peace, love and the other fruit of the Spirit as much as possible as you are suffering. It is holding onto your faith and values and maintaining a positive attitude without blaming God. This is the example of Job. Although Job got angry and complained about his suffering, he maintained his dignity and integrity by living right, seeking God, and not cursing God (Job 1:20-22, 2:9-10, 42:7-10).

It has been said that the last human freedom is the freedom to choose one's attitude. You can choose to walk in the Spirit or walk in the flesh. You can choose to help others or just help yourself. You can choose to serve God and do His will or become angry and depressed. You can suffer with a bad attitude and a defeatist spirit or you can suffer with a good attitude and a victorious spirit. You can choose to follow Christ or to follow this world. Suffering is the great furnace of affliction that can bring out the best in you or the worst in you, that can draw you closer to God or cause you to deny God, and it is your decision what you will do. God is watching you in your suffering; do not disappoint Him.

It is the way that you take up your cross that suffering can have great meaning. It is resolving to suffer honorably, not miserably or shamefully. It is resolving to honor God and to turn your suffering into triumph by maintaining your faith in God and following Christ. It is enduring suffering with dignity that will give you the opportunity to find meaning in life, and helplessness, lack of purpose, lack of achievement, or lack of enjoyment cannot detract from the dignity of this suffering.

Suffering can lead us to greater meaning in several ways, but the foundation for finding meaning through suffering is that suffering places us in a position to experience God. If you follow Christ and seek God in your suffering, you will experience God. When you experience God, you will know God in a greater way and feel more connected to Him, and when you know God in a greater way and feel more connected to Him, life has greater meaning for you.

Before I extol the virtues of suffering, however, I must share that suffering is not meant to be a continuous exercise with no ending (although there are people who have to live with handicaps and thorns for the rest of their lives). The Bible says that hope deferred makes the heart sick (Prov 13:12), and this is very true. If you are in a continuous state of suffering and can never find relief, you will become sick emotionally. There is a time for everything and a time for every purpose under heaven (Eccl 3:1-8). There is a time to cry and a time to mourn, but there is also a time to laugh

53

and a time to dance. God allows suffering to come to us for a purpose, but there is a time when this season of suffering will end and we come to the other side. Even Job's suffering came to an end. Therefore, when I extol the virtues of suffering for finding greater meaning in life, have this balance in mind.

Suffering can lead us to greater meaning in the following ways. First, suffering can show you if your life has been meaningless and what is true meaning. Suffering can help you see what is important in life and to set your priorities right. Suffering can shake up your life so that you can see yourself or a situation better in order to make changes. Suffering can help you see the will of God for your life. Seeing all these things can enable you to make the right decisions and the necessary changes for your life so that you can find greater meaning for your life.

Second, suffering can force us to seek God and His righteousness. This can be an initial seeking of God or drawing closer to God. When you draw close to God, God draws close to you. When you seek God with all of your heart and are willing to see the truth, God will reveal Himself and His ways to you. When God reveals Himself to you, you have experienced and your life has greater meaning.

Third, suffering can be the tool for helping you become a better person and forming good character in you if you persevere through suffering in righteousness and with the right attitude (Rom 5:3-5, James 1:2-4). This is why we are exhorted to see suffering as discipline from God (Heb 12:5-13), for suffering can bring change and healing to us. When you see change and improvement in your character or healing in your soul, you have experienced God and your life has greater meaning.

The greatest way that you can become a better person and be more like Christ is by dying to self, and the only way you can die to self is by going through suffering. Suffering humbles you and gets out the pride. Suffering purifies the heart by forcing you to lay down what is not good and to resolve to do what is right. Suffering forces you to examine yourself and your life and see what kind of person you are and what direction you are heading. Suffering enables you to see your weak and strong points so that you can improve your weaknesses and build upon your strengths. Suffering can make you stronger if you let it, and if you have ever suffered greatly for an extended period of time, when the suffering is over, you realize there is nothing more to fear in life, except to fear God.

Fourth, suffering can force you to trust God in a greater way and to draw upon the Spirit of God for strength. When you trust God, God is there for you, and the more you need God, the more God is there for you, giving you the help, strength, and comfort that you need. Thus, the greater the suffering you go through, the greater the power and presence of God you can experience (2Cor 1:5). Our primary concern when we are suffering is to be delivered from this suffering, we just want to get out of it, but God's primary concern is that we trust in Him and know Him in a greater way and draw upon Him (His grace) for strength and comfort.

It is our lot in this world to endure suffering and to be persecuted for Christ and righteousness, although sometimes this suffering is more than we can endure and should endure, but the Lord helps us through whatever suffering we are in, especially if we call upon Him and draw upon His Spirit. When you see how God has helped you in your suffering, you will have experienced God. You will then know God in a greater way and feel more connected to Him, and life will have greater meaning for you. This should be the testimony of all who follow the Lord.

God will even bring you into a position where you cannot rely upon yourself but must rely upon Him. The apostle Paul was in this position one time. He said,

"⁸We do not want you to be uninformed, brothers and sisters, about the troubles we experienced in the province of Asia. We were under great pressure, far beyond our ability to endure, so that we despaired of life itself. ⁹Indeed, we felt we had received the sentence of death. But this happened that we might not rely on ourselves but on God, who raises the dead. ¹⁰He has delivered us from such a deadly peril, and he will deliver us again. On him we have set our hope that he will continue to deliver us, ¹¹as you help us by your prayers" (2Cor 1:8-11a, NIV, see 1:3-11).

Paul testified how God put him in a situation where he could not rely upon himself but had to rely upon God. This forced him and his companions to draw their comfort and strength from God and to hope in Him for deliverance. This comfort and strength is available to everyone who needs it and it is available no matter what situation you are in or what you have done.

This truth was witnessed by even those who suffered in the concentration camps of World War II. Corrie ten Boom, a Christian, whose family was imprisoned because they were hiding Jews from the Nazis, tells how she and her sister made an effort to minister to others in the death camp. They held Bible studies and prayer groups and saw God move in the hearts of the women, and many found Christ or were strengthened in their faith.

Her ministry after the war was inspired by what her sister Betsie had said to her in the camp just before she died. She told Corrie, "We must tell people what we have learned here. We must tell them that there is no pit so deep that He is not deeper still. They will listen to us, Corrie, because we have been here."[7] When you are in a pit, pray for deliverance, but also pray for courage, strength, and protection to do the will of God in that situation. When you draw upon the power of God in a deeper and greater way and do the will of God for helping people and reaching people for Christ, you will experience God, and when you experience God in this way, you will know God in a more intimate way and life has greater meaning.

Fifth, suffering can bring you into greater union with Christ if you suffer for Him and the righteousness of God. This suffering enables you to experience the most intimate union with God, for the Spirit of glory rests upon you (1Pet 4:12-14), and when you experience God in this way, you know where you are going when you die and life has greater meaning. Jesus said,

"[10]Blessed are those who are persecuted because of righteousness, for theirs is the kingdom of heaven. [11]Blessed are you when people insult you, persecute you and falsely say all kinds of evil against you because of me. [12]Rejoice and be glad, because great is your reward in heaven, for in the same way they persecuted the prophets who were before you" (Matt 5:10-12, NIV; cf. Matt 10:16-39, Rom 8:17-23, Phi 1:29, 3:7-11, 2Thes 1:4-5, 2Tim 1:8, 2:3-10, 3:10-13, Heb 2:17-18, 1Pet 2:20b-21, 3:17, 4:1, 4:12-19, 5:9).

---

7- Corrie ten Boom, with John and Elizabeth Sherrill, *The Hiding Place* (Old Tappan, NJ: Fleming H. Revell, 1971, rpt. Bantam Books, 1975), p. 217.

Suffering for Christ can involve three aspects. First, suffering for Christ is being persecuted for Him because you are His follower. Second, suffering for Christ is being persecuted for righteousness because you are living by godly morals and values. Third, suffering for Christ is going through any kind of suffering or hardship by trusting God and following Jesus, finding your comfort and strength in God and being true to Christ. This third kind of suffering might be called persecution from the kingdom of darkness and this world. Whenever you suffer by trusting God and following Christ and the righteousness of God, you are suffering for your faith in Christ, and God will reward you.

When we suffer for Christ, we identify with Him and this is a testimony to others, and as we suffer with dignity and integrity, we bring glory to God. This kind of suffering has nothing to do with God wanting to improve your character (although it can make you a better person). The suffering that Job went through had nothing to do with God wanting to teach him something. Job was tested as a testimony to the spiritual hosts of light and darkness in order to show forth the glory of God (Job 1:6-12, 2:1-6), and although Job was not perfect in his suffering, he still passed the test and God rewarded him (Job 42:1-10). You do not have to be perfect in your suffering in order to pass the test and be rewarded by God. You do not even have to like your suffering. Job did not like his suffering. You do not have to be perfect; just be consistent (consistently good), and when you fail, get up and go forward again.

Finally, how can we endure suffering? First, you can endure suffering by trusting God and putting your life and everything else in His hands, which includes resolving to live in His peace and joy. This is letting go and giving the situation to God. Second, you can endure suffering by focusing on knowing God. We want to get out of suffering more than anything else, but God wants us to know Him more than anything else. While God wants you to pray for deliverance, your primary focus should be to know God. Third, you can endure suffering through loving contemplation of a loved one. One's earthly family and loved ones can be included here, but let your primary focus of love be God and the death on the cross for your sins by Jesus Christ. Fourth, you can endure suffering by being responsible to someone or something. You can be responsible to finish an unfinished work or to be with loved ones who need you or to fulfill what God has called you to do. Fifth, you can endure suffering by having hope of the future. If you have eternal life in Christ, then you know you have a good future. For this life God always has plans to give you a good future, but you must see His love (Rom 8:28-39) and you may need revelation for a new direction.

Sixth, and lastly, you can endure suffering by making a sacrifice and having selfless goals. The greatest sacrifice and selfless goal is to take the focus off of yourself and your problems and focus on what God wants or expects of you in the situation. You can either focus on your suffering or submit yourself to God and focus on doing His will, helping others, and fulfilling your mission in life. God is watching over you in your suffering; you must not disappoint Him.

We can find the greatest meaning in life through suffering, for suffering reveals what is important in life and draws us closer to God. What life means to you and what gives you meaning in life will be found by what you are willing to suffer for and even to die for. What are you willing to suffer for? This reveals your why for living and what gives you meaning in life. Remember, however, that God is asking you: Will you make Me your meaning in life?

## Summary: The Search for Meaning

A. Defining meaning: Meaning is the why of life. Why am I living and what makes life worth living for me?

B. How you find meaning:
1. Living for a cause that is greater than you and will help people. Will your cause be the gospel of Jesus Christ?
2. Living for someone who is greater than you or dear to you. Will that greater and dearer someone be God through Jesus Christ?
3. Feeling socially connected to your world. Will you love God and others? (Commandment: Loving God and loving others)
4. Having peace with the eight questions of meaning (divinity, origin, being, purpose, worth, evil, morality, and destiny).
5. Making God the foundation for finding meaning in life.

C. How you can discover greater meaning:
1. Performing a selfless deed to help others or accomplishing something that requires much effort and faith.
2. Experiencing a value through another person, developing a value through your actions, or receiving a revelation of a value.
3. Suffering. The principles to find meaning through suffering are:
1) Suffering enables you to see what is meaningful in life.
2) You must find meaning in suffering or your life has no meaning.
3) What you are willing to suffer for is what gives you meaning.
4) You find meaning when you suffer with dignity and by honoring God.
5) Suffering enables you to find meaning by experiencing God in a greater way. You can experience God by seeing what is important in life and making changes, drawing closer to God, building character, trusting God, and suffering for Christ

D. How we can endure suffering: 1) trusting God, 2) focusing on knowing God, 3) loving God and others, 4) being responsible to your duties, 5) having hope of the future, and 6) having selfless goals by thinking about others and doing the will of God.

**Chapter 3**

# The Search for Purpose

We have a tremendous need for purpose, and so there is a search for purpose. While purpose and meaning are used many times as synonyms and it could be said that purpose belongs in the realm of meaning (as was seen in the search for Meaning), purpose is so significant that it must be examined by itself. Once you have found meaning in life (the why for living), purpose is how you will fulfill this meaning. Purpose involves what you do, the relationships you have, and the use of your time. Having purpose is believing or feeling that you are living life to the fullest in what you work at, who you relate to, and how you spend your time.

We must find purpose in life in order to find fulfillment. We desperately search for purpose, for purpose gives us direction in life and a reason for living. If you do not have purpose in life, you will be driven by negative forces, forces from the outside (people and this world) who pull on you to conform you into their image and forces from within (emptiness, pain, bitterness, fear, anxiety, worry, guilt, depression, loneliness) that will drive you to unhealthy and dysfunctional behavior in order to find fulfillment.

If you live without purpose, you will live an unfulfilled life with wasted potential, and you will battle emptiness and discouragement every day of your life. If you live without purpose, the smallest obstacles and problems will seem like mountains too great to climb. Purpose gives you strength and perseverance for overcoming obstacles and adversity so that you can set your face like flint through every trial and tribulation and have the patience to run the marathon race of life. This life will wear you down and break your heart and cause you to want to quit, but having purpose will keep you going and give you a reason for getting up in the morning. Purpose will give you the strength to endure the greatest trials and keep you steady through the storms of life, but without purpose, the slightest wind will put fear in your heart and the smallest problem or obstacle will become a great weight so that life becomes a burden to bear rather than an experience to enjoy.

What is purpose? Purpose is the how of life; it is what you do and how you spend your time. Purpose is what you set before yourself as an object to be attained or accomplished. Purpose is having a goal in mind, an end in view, with the aim and intention of reaching or obtaining this goal. Thus, the essence of purpose is having a goal that one works toward. This goal might have an end or it might be something that you do on a continuous basis because it fulfills you. A goal can be an individual task (and this can include relationships) or a work that has many tasks or a vocation or calling that is a never ending work (and this can include marriage). It is even possible for a work to be one's mission in life and the reason for one's existence. Finding purpose, therefore, comes by making a commitment to a goal and then working and persevering to attain or accomplish this goal.

There are three areas in life where we find purpose- work, relationships, self improvement. We find purpose by: 1) engaging in fulfilling work and activities that will utilize one's gifts, abilities, and motivations, 2) having meaningful relationships that will enable one to love and to be loved and to be part of a family, and 3) improving oneself by developing one's gifts, abilities, and character so that one is able to reach one's full potential and become a mature person. These are the three basic ways that we find purpose in life. If you set these things before you as goals and work toward them, you will find purpose.

There is also purpose from a spiritual perspective. We find purpose through ministry (work in the Church) and missions (work to reach the world for Christ). We find purpose through worship (relationship with God) and fellowship (relationship with fellow believers). We find purpose through discipleship (becoming more like Christ). We minister to fellow believers and the world (work). We love God and the family of God (relationships). We become more like Christ (self improvement). These five purposes of the spiritual life fit into the three basic purposes described above.

Many people are focused on finding one's place in life or finding out who you are, and this will be their concern and what they talk about. This is a natural desire, and for a lot of people this may be their focus when searching for purpose, but understand that you will find your place in life and find out who you are when you work toward satisfying the three basic purposes of life. You will find yourself when you find fulfilling work and meaningful relationships and are improving yourself.

We find purpose when we find satisfaction and a sense of accomplishment through what we do and who we are with and how we spend our time, whether it is completing a task, passing a test, earning money, connecting with others, helping others, or improving your health. Finding purpose, however, is much greater than accomplishing goals in one's work, relationships, or self improvement. You can find fulfilling work and meaningful relationships and be improving yourself and still feel empty and unfulfilled after awhile if there is not a central purpose or a foundational purpose to all your effort and goals.

You must have a foundational purpose for your life, something that will be the focus for your goals. The seeking for fulfilling work, meaningful relationships, and self improvement are all elements for finding purpose, and one can find a certain measure of purpose in these endeavors for a certain amount of time, but the foundation for finding purpose is having a central purpose in life. If you do not have this central purpose, you will not find lasting purpose. You might find purpose for many years, but it will fade away if you do not have a foundational purpose for your life. This foundational purpose is your central mission in life. This is the foundation for purpose.

This foundational purpose must be a purpose that is permanent and unchanging. How you find purpose in fulfilling work, meaningful relationships, and improving yourself can change, but your foundational purpose never changes. It is a greater purpose that keeps you persevering toward your goals of work, relationships, and self improvement. This foundational purpose will not allow you to be satisfied with your accomplishments. This foundational purpose gives you a reason for living that will never go away and will not allow you to give up on life, whether it is not wanting to live anymore or withdrawing from life. This foundational purpose enables you to die to self so that you are able to make sacrifices and give yourself to this greater purpose.

This foundational purpose could be called your meaning in life, but it is not quite this. It is the link between meaning and purpose. Meaning is the why of life, whereas purpose is the how of life. How will you live for God and give yourself to the cause of the gospel of Jesus Christ? How will you love God and others and become like Christ? These are the questions for finding purpose. Your foundational purpose, however, describes your heart attitude as you walk out your meaning in life and fulfill your purpose. Your foundational purpose, therefore, is finding the heart attitude that will enable you to live wholly for God and give yourself totally to the cause of the gospel of Jesus Christ.

In the search for meaning it was seen that you find meaning by giving yourself to a cause that is greater than you and living your life for a person who is greater than you. It is also to love God and others. Whoever you live for and whatever cause you give your life to, this is your life mission. This life mission can be called purpose or meaning, for your life mission is where meaning and purpose come together. The cause you give your life to and the person you live for is your meaning in life. Purpose is how you will give your life to this cause and how you will live for this person. Purpose also includes the heart attitude for this life mission. This is your foundational purpose. This foundational purpose drives your general purposes in life (work, relationships, self improvement) for fulfilling your life mission and is permanent and unchanging.

This foundational purpose- the heart attitude that enables you to live for someone and give yourself to a cause- will be the focus and subject of this chapter. This chapter will not include finding purpose through fulfilling work, meaningful relationships, and self improvement. These three purposes are significant in themselves and require their own study. They will be examined separately in the search for Achievement (work), the search for Love (relationships), and the search for Maturity (self improvement).

What exactly is this foundational purpose for life? When you give yourself to a cause that is greater than you and commit yourself to a person (or a people) who you will live your life for, the only way you can do this the right way is by dying to self. Dying to self is placing the interests of the cause and another before your own interests. If you cannot die to self in this way, then the cause and others will merely become instruments to promote yourself and your own agenda and interests. The sin problem in the human race is rooted in pride, lifting oneself up and looking out for self. Therefore, the foundational purpose must be expressed in such a way that it helps you die to self so that you can get rid of your pride and humble yourself and give yourself wholly to that cause and make a total commitment to that person.

## Section 3B: Finding Purpose

Jesus had something to say about living for someone and a cause and how to find purpose in life. He said,

"$^{24}$If anyone desires to come after Me, let him deny himself, and take up his cross, and follow Me. $^{25}$For whoever desires to save his life will lose it, but whoever desires to lose his life for My sake will find it. $^{26}$For what does a man profit if he gains the whole world, and loses his soul? Or what will a man give in exchange for his soul?" (Matt 16:24-26, NKJV; cf. Matt 10:37-39, Mark 8:34-37, Luke 9:23-25, Luke 14:26-27,33 {"be My disciple"} & Luke 17:33, John 12:24-26).

Purpose and fulfillment is in Jesus Christ. Jesus said that if you wanted to come after Him and be His disciple, you had to deny yourself and carry your cross and follow Him. This teaching was given in the context of His own suffering and death on the cross (Matt 16:21-23). What does it mean to deny self and take up your cross and follow Jesus? Denying self is putting aside your wants and desires and placing God and His will first. Carrying your cross is humbling yourself and surrendering to God and doing the will of God no matter what the cost is. Following Jesus is making Him Lord of your life and following His life and teachings. Denying self and carrying your cross and following Jesus is dying to self.

Dying to self is losing sight of self and seeing Christ as your life. Dying to self is seeing Christ and the kingdom of God as being far greater and much more valuable than you and giving your heart to what is worth more. It is the hidden treasure found in a field and the pearl of great price (Matt 13:44-45).

Dying to self is making a choice. Even though you have been crucified with Christ (Rom 6:4-6, Gal 2:20), you still must choose to deny self, carry your cross, and follow Jesus (Luke 9:23, Rom 6:11-13). You must choose every day to put down pride and get rid of the big "I" and humble yourself and develop a humble spirit. You must choose every day to submit your mind, will, and emotions to Christ and follow Him as Lord and do the will of God.

The middle verse in this passage (verse 25) expounds upon this idea of dying to self. Jesus said that you must "lose your life for My sake". The Greek word "*apollumi*", in the passive voice here, means "to lose, perish, be destroyed" and indicates total destruction or loss (cf. Luke 15:24, 17:29, John 3:16, 17:12). Jesus used this word to bring out the concept of the total death of self.

It must be noted that this teaching of Matthew 16:25 is quoted six times in the Gospels with each having different wordings. If you have had much experience as a teacher or preacher, you know that you might use different points and words for different audiences, depending upon your focus for a particular audience. Jesus did a lot of teaching and preaching and did the same thing.[1] The different words that are used in these references help bring out the full meaning of this statement about losing one's life for Christ. These six verses are listed below.

(Matt 10:39)- "He who finds his life will lose it, and he who loses his life for My sake will find it" (NKJV; "find"- *eurisko*, SC-#2147; cf. Matt 7:7,8, 11:29, 17:27; "lose"- *apollumi*, SC-#622, also in Matt 16:25, Mark 8:35, Luke 9:24, 17:33, John 12:25).

(Matt 16:25)- "For whoever desires to save his life will lose it, and whoever loses his life for My sake will find it" (NKJV; "save"- *sozo*, SC-#4982; "find"- *eurisko*; cf. Matt 8:25, 9:21, 10:22, 24:13,22,42, Mark 5:23,28, 6:56, 10:52, Luke 7:50, 8:36,48,50, 17:19, John 11:12, 12:27, Acts 4:9, 7:25, 14:9, 27:20, James 5:15).

(Mark 8:35)- "For whoever desires to save his life will lose it, but whoever loses his life for My sake and the gospel's will save it" (NKJV; "save"- *sozo*; cf. Mark 10:21).

---

1- For example, different words are used in the context of the cross of Christ (Matt 16:21-23, Mark 8:31-33, Luke 9:21-22, John 12:23,27-33) and the context of persecution and the last days (Matt 10:16-37, Luke 17:26-32).

(Luke 9:24)- "For whoever desires to <u>save</u> his life will lose it, but whoever loses his life for My sake will <u>save</u> it" (NKJV; "save"- *sozo*; Note: This verse is the same as Mark 8:35 except that it does not have "and the gospel's").

(Luke 17:33)- "Whoever seeks to <u>save</u> his life will lose it, and whoever loses his life will <u>preserve</u> it" (NKJV; see Luke 14:26,27,33; "save"- *sozo*; "preserve"- *zoogoneo*, SC-#2225, and is also translated as "keep" with the root meaning of "make alive, keep alive", cf. Acts 7:19).

(John 12:25)- "He who <u>loves</u> his life will lose it, and he who <u>hates</u> his life in this world will <u>keep</u> it for eternal life" (NKJV; "loves"- *phileo*, SC-#5368; "hates"- *miseo*, SC-#3404; cf. Luke 14:26; "keep"- *phulasso*, SC-#5442, and is also translated as "preserve" with the root meaning of "guard, keep safe, keep watch", cf. Luke 2:8, 11:28, 18:21, John 17:12, 2Tim 1:12,14).

These verses are not just speaking about eternal life (although the passage in John highlights eternal life). They are also speaking about life in this world. You can never separate salvation for eternal life from salvation or wholeness for this life, for we enter the kingdom of God as soon as we are born of the Spirit (John 3:3-8). We have been saved (through confession of Christ), we are being saved (by following Christ), and we will be saved (when we are glorified at the return of Christ). We have been redeemed, but the Bible also says that our redemption will not be made complete until the return of Christ.[2]

We are born of the Spirit and have entered into the kingdom of God through faith in Jesus Christ (Eph 1:7,14, Col 1:13-14), but we have not yet been made perfect and must die to self and follow Jesus in order to overcome temptation, sin, suffering, the flesh, the world, and the forces of darkness.[3] If you do not follow Jesus and stay on the right path, you will reap pain and sorrow in your soul

---

2- Cf. 2Cor 1:10 and 2Tim 4:17-18. We have been redeemed (Eph 1:7,14, Col 1:13-14). We are being conformed into the image of Christ (Rom 8:29, 2Cor 3:18). We are waiting for redemption (Luke 21:28, Rom 8:23, Eph 1:14, 4:30).
3- Cf. Matt 10:22, Gal 5:19-25, Phi 2:12-13, Eph 6:10-18, 1Tim 4:16, 6:11-12, 2Tim 2:20-22, 4:7-8, Heb 3:12-14, Rev 2:7,11,17,26, 3:5,11,12,21, 21:7.

and destruction in your life. This should be self evident.

The Bible expresses the importance of persevering in your salvation, for it is by persevering in your salvation and standing firm in your faith that you will be saved. In the passages where Jesus only uses the word "save", He might be focusing only on salvation for eternal life, but in the other passages where He uses "find" or "preserve (keep alive)" or "keep (guard)", He seems to be including finding wholeness in your soul for this life as well as finding salvation for eternal life.[4]

We also see this element of finding wholeness for the soul in this life through Christ in the use of the word *psyche*. This Greek word is translated as "life" in Matthew 16:25, but it is better translated as "soul", which is how it is translated in the following verse (verse 26). This word indicates a living being, the breath of life, one's whole being, and the seat of personality (the mind, will, and emotions). It is the inner being or inner self and can include the spirit (Matt 10:28, Acts 2:41), although it can be distinguished from the spirit (1Thes 5:23, Heb 4:12). The soul is where the spirit and the flesh meet, which is considered to be the mind.[5]

Whereas the Greek word *zoe*, which means "life", indicates having life in contrast to physical or spiritual death and is the word that is used in the context of eternal life (John 12:25), the word *psyche* indicates the inner self or the soul (the mind, will, and emotions). This use of *psyche* (which focuses on the inner self) and the use of words like "find", "preserve (keep alive)", and "keep (guard)" indicate that Jesus is speaking about keeping your soul whole in this world as well as for eternal life.

---

4- Cf. "save (*sozo*)" (SC-#4982)- Matt 10:22, 24:13, Mark 3:4, Luke 6:9, Acts 2:40, 1Cor 1:18, 15:2, 1Tim 4:16, James 1:21, 2:14, 1Pet 4:18; "salvation (*soteria*)" (SC-#4991)- Rom 13:11, 2Cor 1:6, 7:10, Phi 2:12, 2Tim 3:15, Heb 6:9, 9:28, 1Pet 1:5,9, 2:2, Rev 12:10; the "if" statements- 1Cor 15:2, Col 1:22-23a, Heb 3:6, 3:12-14.

5- In other verses, *psyche* (SC-#5590, *psuche*) is translated as "life" (Matt 10:39, Mark 8:35, Luke 9:24, 14:26, 17:33, John 12:25) and "soul" (Mark 8:36). Luke 9:25 says "is himself destroyed (*apollumi*) or lost (*zemioo*)" (NKJV) or "loses or forfeits his very self" (NIV). The verb *apollumi* (SC-#622), in the passive voice, means "to be destroyed, perish" (Matt 10:39, 16:25, Mark 8:35, Luke 9:24,25, 17:33, John 12:25; John 3:15,16). The verb *zemioo* (SC-#2210), in the passive, means "to lose, suffer loss" (Matt 16:26, Mark 8:36, Luke 9:26; 1Cor 3:15, Phi 3:8). The word "himself (*eautou*)" (SC-#1438) = third person reflexive pronoun.

Let us now examine the full meaning of this passage using the text of Matthew 10:39, which uses only "find" in each clause.

"He who finds his life (*psyche*) will lose it, and he who loses his life (*psyche*) for My sake will find it" (Matt 10:39, NKJV).

What does it mean to try to find your life or soul? Wanting to find your life or soul is trying to find happiness and wholeness in yourself and this world. This includes loving your life in this world and being a lover of the things of this world more than being a lover of God. It is trying to find purpose, fulfillment, and happiness by seeking to please self and following after the desires of self.

One of the features of the 1960's "Me Generation" was the focus to find oneself. People were saying, "I need to find myself". This meant that you were trying to find out who you are and what you wanted to do in life. But when you seek to find yourself through yourself and in your own power, you end up in nothingness, and this is what happened to this generation. They followed a path that did not lead to true and lasting fulfillment, leaving a godless legacy to the following generations. It is by seeking God and His ways through His Son Jesus Christ that you find yourself.

Jesus said that if you try to find your life, if you try to find wholeness, purpose, fulfillment, and happiness in yourself and through this world, you will lose your soul. What does it mean to lose your soul? Losing your soul means to not find inner wholeness, but, instead, to end up with inner pain. Losing your soul means to not find lasting purpose and fulfillment, but, instead, to end up with emptiness. Furthermore, if you refuse to follow Jesus, then you will not just lose your soul for this life, but you will also lose your soul for eternal life.

In Matthew 16:26 Jesus asked two existential questions: "What will it profit you to gain the whole world but lose your soul?" and "What can you give in exchange for your soul?" If you exchange following Jesus or your morals and values in order to gain power, fame, money, or pleasure (Luke 8:14-15, 21:34-36), you are in essence selling your soul for something that is not God and has only temporary worth. You are chasing the wind (that which is nothing) and will end up reaping the whirlwind (that which is destruction). If you continue down this path and do not turn away to follow the right path, you will lose your soul. You will lose your soul in this life by losing the life of God in you and having total emptiness, and if you do not repent, you will lose your soul for eternal life. You do not want to gain the whole world but lose your soul, for in the end you gain nothing and lose everything.

"He who finds his life (*psyche*) will lose it, and he who loses his life (*psyche*) for My sake will find it" (Matt 10:39, NKJV).

What does it mean to lose your life for Christ? Jesus stated in the previous verse that it was by denying self and carrying your cross and following Him (Matt 10:38; see Matt 16:24, Mark 8:34, Luke 9:23, 14:27,33, John 12:26). Losing your life for Christ is trying to find wholeness, purpose, and fulfillment in Christ. You disdain your life in this world because you see that this world is in bondage to sin and the kingdom of darkness and is only temporary (Matt 6:33, 13:44-46, John 15:19, 2Cor 4:18, 6:14-18, Col 3:1-3, Heb 11:13-40, James 4:4, 1John 2:15-17, 5:19, Rev 12:11). You see that you are only a pilgrim in this world and desire the kingdom of God more than this world, knowing that Christ is the door to the kingdom of God.

Therefore, losing your life for Christ is finding wholeness, purpose, and fulfillment by denying self, taking up your cross, and following Christ. You deny self by humbling yourself and laying down your wants and desires and putting God first. You take up and carry your cross by surrendering to God and doing the will of God no matter what the cost is (just as Christ obeyed God in carrying His cross). You follow Jesus by making Him Lord of your life and following His life and the commandments of God and knowing that your life is now in Him. When you deny self and carry your cross and follow Jesus, this is dying to self. You lose sight of self and set your eyes upon Christ and see Him as your life, having in your heart- "Thy kingdom come, Thy will be done." It is no longer you anymore; it is now Jesus. Jesus said,

"Most assuredly, I say to you, unless a grain of wheat falls into the ground and dies, it remains alone; but if it dies, it produces much grain" (John 12:24, NKJV).

The above verse is the preceding verse in the corresponding passage in John. Jesus is stating a principle that applies to everyone, and points to His death on the cross. He is saying that in order for a seed to grow into a plant that produces fruit or stalks of grain, it must first die. The same is true for the spiritual life. If you want to be changed and have the life of God in you, you must die. When you receive Christ in your heart, you are co-crucified and co-buried with Christ, the old nature being put to death, and then you are raised up in union with Christ with the new nature (Rom 6:3-18, Gal 2:20-21, Col 2:12, Acts 20:24). This is the born again experience. When you are born of the Spirit, you will grow spiritually and produce fruit for the kingdom of God (Matt 13:18-23, John 15:8,16), but, as will be explained later, you must also choose every day to die to self, to put down pride and develop a humble spirit and be submitted to God. This seed that Jesus is talking about, this seed that must first die to produce life, is your life and represents dying to self and losing one's life for Christ.

"He who finds his life (*psyche*) will lose it, and he who loses his life (*psyche*) for My sake will find it" (Matt 10:39, NKJV).

Jesus said that if you lose your life for Him, trying to find your life in Him, you will find your life or soul. What does it mean to find your life or soul in Christ? Finding your life or soul means that you find wholeness for your soul and that you find lasting purpose and fulfillment. It is finding peace, joy, love, faith, and hope, and although these virtues will be tested, you always have a wellspring and fountain that you can tap into. Finding your life is keeping your soul spiritually filled and guarding your soul from darkness and oppression. It is finding life in the Spirit for this life and the life to come.

Losing your life for Christ and finding your life in Him will lead you to find purpose, and this will be the foundational purpose for your life. This is your foundational purpose, and having this as your foundation will enable you to find lasting purpose and fulfillment in life.

This was the foundational purpose for the apostle Paul. His consuming passion was to lose his life for Christ so that he might better know Christ. He said,

"[7]But whatever was to my profit I now consider loss for the sake of Christ. [8]What is more, I consider everything a loss compared to the surpassing greatness of knowing Christ Jesus my Lord, for whose sake I have lost all things. I consider them rubbish, that I may gain Christ [9]and be found in him, not having a righteousness of my own that comes from the law, but that which is through faith in Christ-the righteousness that comes from God and is by faith. [10]I want to know Christ and the power of his resurrection and the fellowship of sharing in his sufferings, becoming like him in his death, [11]and so, somehow, to attain to the resurrection from the dead" (Phi 3:7-11, NIV; *summorphoo* (SC-#4833)- "becoming like").

Paul said that he had lost everything to follow Christ, and considered what he had lost as garbage compared to knowing Christ and being made righteous through faith in Him (3:7-9). Paul continues by saying that his overwhelming desire now was to know Christ and the power of His resurrection and the fellowship of His sufferings, being conformed to His death or becoming like Him in his death (3:10).

How does one become like Christ in His death? It is by dying to self. In the previous chapter Paul described how Christ humbled Himself to become a human being and a servant and was obedient unto death on the cross (Phi 2:5-8). This is dying to self, and this is what Paul was striving for. Paul wanted to die to self as Christ had died to self on the cross. Paul saw dying to self and losing his life for Christ as the way to knowing Christ and becoming more like Christ and having the power of God. This was his purpose in life and what brought him the greatest fulfillment. Furthermore, he believed that dying to self like Christ would be the means by which he might somehow "attain to the resurrection out from the dead" (literal translation).

Now, if this is speaking about a physical resurrection from the dead, how can dying to self like Christ in His death enable you to attain or have a better chance of attaining the resurrection of the dead? This is a strange statement, and it is not meant to be hypothetical, for Paul is making a true claim to attain this. This statement is also contrary to sound doctrine, for we are assured of the resurrection of the dead in Christ (1Cor 15:12-23,35-58), a point that Paul makes evident a few verses later (Phi 3:20-21).

Is Paul saying that if he dies to self, he can make his salvation more secure?[6] Paul does teach that we must persevere in our salvation, but the resurrection of the body could not be the focus if he was talking about the perseverance of salvation. He uses the expression "from (*ek*) the dead" and not "of the dead". If he had used "of the dead", this would imply the future physical resurrection of the dead, but using "from the dead" implies a resurrection that can occur in this life (cf. Matt 14:2, 28:7, Rom 1:4, 10:9, Eph 1:19-20 vs. Matt 22:31, 1Cor 15:12-13).[7] The meaning of this clause can be brought to light by examining the Greek word that is translated here as "resurrection".

The Greek word that is translated as "resurrection" is *exanastasis*.[8] This is derived from *anastasis*, which means "resurrection, rising up" and is the standard term for indicating the resurrection of the dead (Matt 27:53, Luke 20:36, John 11:24-25, Rom 1:4, 6:5, 1Cor 15:42, Phi 3:10). Paul had just used this term in the previous verse to refer to the resurrection from the dead of Christ, but now he uses the derivative *exanastasis* (only used here in the Greek Bible), which literally means "out-resurrection" or

---

6- Paul introduces this sentence with the phrase *ei pos* (SC-#1513), which means "if by any means, if possibly, if somehow" (cf. Acts 27:12, Rom 1:10, 11:14). This phrase is called a conditional expression, suggesting that the attainment of something is possible but not certain or that it is not altogether within the subject's power or ability and will require God's help.

7- For this clause the Greek text of the KJV/NKJV (*ten exanastasin ton nekron*) is different from the Greek text of the NASB/NIV (*ten exanastasin ten ek nekron*). Although the NKJV reads "the resurrection from the dead", the KJV reads "the resurrection of the dead" and is based upon the second article (*ton*) in the Greek text being plural genitive with the absence of the preposition *ek* (from). This means that this phrase would be translated with "of" and that "dead (*nekros*)" (SC-#3498, adj.) is plural, indicating the future physical resurrection of the dead. However, the KJV Greek text (Textus Receptus) still uses *exanastasis*, which must be translated as "resurrection out". Therefore, the true translation would be "the resurrection out of the dead", which really has the same meaning as "the resurrection out from the dead". The Textus Receptus for this phrase (trying to smooth out a difficult phrase) is considered an inferior text.

8- The noun *exanastasis* (SC-#1815) is derived from *anastasis* (SC-#386) by the addition of the prefix *ek/ex* (SC-#1537), which means "out, from, out of, away from" and is used to signify the separation of an item that had been in or with something. The corresponding verb *exanistemi* (SC-#1817) is derived from *anistemi* (SC-#450). *Anistemi* means "to raise up" or "to rise, arise, get up" (Acts 9:39,40, John 11:23,24,31, Rom 15:12, Eph 5:14, 1Thes 4:14,16).

"resurrection out". This coming out of something is what this word signifies. The corresponding verb is *exanistemi* (much more common in Greek literature) and means "to rise up, raise up" with the sense of rising up from among others (Acts 15:5) or coming forth out of another (Mark 12:19, Luke 20:28). Therefore, this phrase must be translated as "the resurrection out from the dead", which is a wording that is never used for indicating a physical resurrection of the dead.

What is Paul trying to say when he says that he hopes to "attain to the resurrection out from the dead"? Paul had introduced this statement by expressing how he had lost his life for Christ and wanted to be like Christ in His death, to die to self as Christ died to self. He then uses *exanastasis* with the preposition *ek* (from) after having used *anastasis* in the previous verse to signify the physical resurrection of Christ. It appears, therefore, that Paul is not speaking about a future physical resurrection but a present spiritual resurrection in Christ.

There is a present spiritual resurrection in Christ. We have been crucified and buried with Christ, signifying that self has been dethroned and the old nature has been put to death (its power has been broken). We then have been resurrected with Christ, signifying that Christ has been enthroned as Lord of one's life and we have been born of the Spirit (born again) and have taken on a new nature that is in the image of Christ. This is Pauline theology (Rom 4:17, 6:3-11, 2Cor 5:17, Gal 2:20, Eph 2:1,4-6, 5:14, Col 2:13, 3:9-11). The essence of the born again experience is making Jesus Christ Savior and Lord so that the old nature dies and the new nature is birthed by the Holy Spirit and your spirit is resurrected into the image of God in Christ.

Paul desired the fullness of this new life in Christ. He wanted to be completely walking in the Spirit and to be totally transformed into the image of Christ. However, he also understood the dichotomy of human nature. While Paul said that he was crucified in Christ and no longer lived but that Christ lives in him (Gal 2:20), he also said that we must live in the Spirit so that we do not gratify the desires of the flesh (Gal 5:16-25).

Paul knew that the new life in Christ is a spiritual transformation where the old nature has been put to death and the new nature has been birthed through the regeneration of the spirit

74

with the reception of the Holy Spirit so that we are able to walk in the Spirit, but he also knew that the flesh (the sin nature) still resides within and can come alive if we do not walk in the Spirit. This is why we are exhorted to walk in the Spirit and not give place to the flesh (Rom 6:12-23, 8:5-17, 13:12-14, Gal 5:16-25). Thus, this new life in Christ is both a present possession and a goal to be pursued (Rom 6:3-23, 12:1-2, Gal 5:16-25, Eph 4:22-24, 5:8-20, Col 3:10).

Paul was teaching in Philippians 3:7-11 that the way to this new life in the Spirit (what he calls the power of the resurrection of Christ) is to lose your life for Christ and die to self as Christ died to self at the cross. When Paul uses the phrase, "the resurrection out from the dead", this was consistent with not only his theology but also his language, for elsewhere he calls the old nature "dead" and refers to the new nature as what has risen or come alive (Rom 6:4,5,11,13, 8:10, Eph 5:14). Thus, when Paul uses the term "dead", he is referring to the old nature (which is dead to spiritual things), and when he uses the phrase "the resurrection out from", he is referring to being so filled with the power of God that the new nature and the anointing of God is what he walks in all the time. Paul wanted to totally live in the new nature and the power and anointing of God, but he saw that losing his life for Christ and dying to self was the pathway for this life in the Spirit.

For Paul, therefore, just as for Christ, death is the gateway to life, and just as Christ taught that dying to self was a path you walked, Paul taught that dying to self was a process. This is supported in the following verses where Paul says that he has not yet fully attained this resurrected life and has not yet been perfected but is pressing on to the goal of the new life in Christ and his calling in Christ Jesus.

"[12]Not that I have already obtained all this, or have already been made perfect, but I press on to take hold of that for which Christ Jesus took hold of me. [13]Brethren, I do not consider myself yet to have taken hold of it. But one thing I do: Forgetting what is behind and straining toward what is ahead, [14]I press on toward the goal to win the prize for which God has called me heavenward in Christ Jesus" (Phi 3:12-14, NIV; cf. Rom 6:11-23).

Paul had lost his life for Christ and was dying to self so that he could become more like Christ and have the power of God manifested in his ministry, but he knew that he had not yet been perfected. He was pressing toward what God had called him to be and what God had called him to do.

This ending statement, and also this entire passage of Scripture (Phi 3:7-14), is a powerful statement that reveals Paul's heart. You can sense and feel a depth and a passion from Paul here. There is a great passion and a deep devotion for Christ. This passion and devotion that comes forth from his heart reveals that he derived great meaning, purpose, and fulfillment from dying to self and losing his life for Christ and pressing toward the heavenly prize and calling that he had in Christ Jesus.

You will find meaning, purpose, and fulfillment when you give yourself to a cause that is greater than you and helps people and when you make a commitment to live your life for someone who is greater than you. The gospel of Jesus Christ is the greatest cause in this world and will help people the most, and living your life for Christ is the greatest commitment that you could ever make. The pathway to this is losing your life for Christ and living for Him. This is also the key for who you should follow. Let your leaders be those who are losing their lives for Christ.

If you want to be successful in anything in life and find purpose, you must give your life to it. The greatest success in the eyes of God and the greatest purpose you can have is to lose your life for Christ. Whether your primary focus for losing your life for Christ is bringing glory to God or loving God or obeying God or doing the will of God or loving people or building the kingdom of God or spreading the gospel, you will find the greatest purpose and fulfillment by making Christ the central mission in your life and the most important thing in your heart.[9]

---

9- For insightful teaching on this passage, see Joni Eareckson-Tada in "To Know Christ and the Power of His Resurrection (Philippians 3:10)", The War Cry (Salvation Army), Easter/April 2001; "Life is Hard...But God is Good", Founder's Week address (Moody Bible Institute), 2/7/1998; 2014 devotionals for March 10 and 28, joniandfriends.org. She also has written several books with a thoughtful analysis on the subjects of suffering and dying to self, doing this from the perspective of being a quadriplegic since the age of 17.

## Section 3C: Losing your Life for Christ

Losing your life for Christ is dying to self and doing the will of God. How do you lose your life for Christ? How do you deny yourself and take up your cross and follow Jesus?

First, you must realize that losing your life for Christ is a work of God. It is what happened at the cross and when you put your faith in Christ. Paul says,

"I have been crucified with Christ; it is no longer I who live but Christ lives in me; and the life which I now live in the flesh I live by faith in the Son of God, who loved me and gave Himself for me" (Gal 2:20, NKJV; "co-crucified"- *sustauroo*, SC-#4957).

"[4]Therefore we were buried with Him through baptism into death, that just as Christ was raised from the dead by the glory of the Father, even so we also should walk in newness of life. [5]For if we have been united together in the likeness of His death, certainly we also shall be in the likeness of His resurrection, [6]knowing this, that our old man was crucified with Him, that the body of sin might be done away with, that we should no longer be slaves of sin. [7]For he who has died has been freed from sin. [8]Now if we died with Christ, we believe that we shall also live with Him" (Rom 6:4-8, NKJV; v.4- "co-buried", *sunthapko*, SC-#4916; v.5- "united", *sumphutos*, SC-#4854; v.6- "co-crucified", *sustauroo*).

Through faith in Christ you have been crucified and buried with Christ and resurrected with Him. This signifies a spiritual transformation (symbolized by baptism). The old nature has been put to death and you have been given a new nature. You have been born of the Spirit. Your spirit has been regenerated and the Holy Spirit resides in you. This might be difficult to comprehend since we have not yet been made perfect and the sin nature still resides in us and the mind must be submitted to the Spirit, but it means that you have the mind of Christ and the power of the flesh (the sin nature) has been broken so that you are no longer in bondage to sin and the evil one and have the ability to walk in the Spirit.

When you professed Christ as your Savior and committed your life to Him as Lord, you really did die with Him. Your old nature died. The use of "co-crucified" (Rom 6:6, Gal 2:20), "co-buried" (Rom 6:4, Col 2:12), and "united" (Rom 6:5) bring out this union with Christ. Moreover, when you died with Christ, you were also resurrected and raised up with Him by the regeneration of your spirit (becoming born of the Spirit) and receiving the Holy Spirit. You are now in union with Christ and have a new life. This means that losing your life for Christ should be a celebration and a pathway to joy. If it is not, something is wrong.

Second, you must realize that losing your life for Christ requires an attitude shift. This attitude shift is that losing your life for Christ brings freedom and is a joyous celebration. Jesus said,

"[28]Come to Me, all you who labor and are heavy laden, and I will give you rest. [29]Take My yoke upon you and learn from Me, for I am gentle and lowly [humble] in heart, and you will find rest for your souls. [30]For My yoke is easy and My burden is light" (Matt 11:28-30, NKJV).[10]

God is not a harsh taskmaster. The Lord relates to us as someone who is meek, gentle, and humble, and the load or requirements we are given are easy and light. The yoke means that God is the boss (for in this world you are yoked to either Christ or Satan). When you are yoked to Christ, God is the boss and you submit yourself to Him, but this yoke is light and not heavy and it is easy and kind and not difficult or harsh. A kind or easy yoke means that the wood is smooth and shaped according to your body and is varnished and padded so that it feels comfortable. It is comfortable because God is helping you out and it is light because God is providing the main power to pull the weight. This life is difficult and tough, but it becomes easier when you place yourself under Christ and put your trust in God.

Therefore, losing your life for Christ should not be some oppressive or depressive lifestyle. It will only seem that way if Jesus is not your Lord or Christ is not your life or you are not

---

10- The Greek word translated as "gentle" means "meek" (*praus*, SC-#4235/4239, adj., note- two spellings). Meekness is power under control and being submitted to God. The Greek word translated as "lowly" means "humble" (*tapeinos*, SC-#5011, adj.). The Greek word translated as "easy" means "kind" (*chrestos*, SC-#5543, adj.), which means that this yoke will not hurt you.

submitted to God or you are walking in pride or want to be in control or are trying to do things in your own power. These are the causes whenever losing your life for Christ becomes a heavy and difficult burden and not a joyous celebration with freedom.

Losing your life for Christ should bring freedom. You are free when you lose your life for Christ. You can now walk in the Spirit and have the power to overcome the flesh, the world, and the kingdom of darkness. This is freedom. You are no longer a slave to these things if you humble yourself and submit yourself to God. You are no longer a slave to self and controlled by selfishness if you live your life for Christ. God came to save us from ourselves, to save us from the big "I" (the ego). When the big "I" is put to death, you are now free to be who God created you to be and to do what has eternal significance and reward.

Losing your life for Christ should be a pathway to joy. When Christ calls you to deny self, carry your cross, and follow Him, this is not supposed to be a sorrowful pathway or an agonizing decision. You are now free to live in the Spirit so that you can experience the peace, joy, and love of God. This is because you are no longer in control but God is in control. When self is in control, you get into trouble and waste your time and do not find peace and fulfillment. When God is in control, you have peace, abundant life, lasting fulfillment, and eternal reward. Therefore, losing your life for Christ should be a joyous celebration. It bonds you with Christ in the most intimate way and leads to peace, blessing, and abundant life in God. This should bring celebration and joy.[11]

We live in a culture where we are so individualistic and self oriented and want self to be in charge, and we do not like authority. We then become so afraid of dying to self. We are so afraid of obeying God. We are so afraid of what He might ask us to do. We are so afraid, but we do not realize that it is by losing your life for Christ (dying to self and obeying God) that you will find wholeness, blessing, purpose, and fulfillment in life. You no longer have to worry about what self wants because self is dead, and dead men have no feelings and no fear.

---

11- For more about how life in Christ is meant to be a joyous celebration, see the ministry of Georgian and Winnie Banov (www.globalcelebration.org).

Third, losing your life for Christ is not just a work of God; it is also a work by you. It is something that you have to make a decision about every day. Jesus said,

"If anyone desires to come after Me, let him deny himself, and take up his cross daily, and follow Me....And whoever does not bear his cross and come after Me cannot be My disciple" (Luke 9:23 and 14:27, NKJV).

Jesus said that you must "take up your cross daily" (Luke 9:23). Paul said that he had to "die daily" in order to endure suffering for Christ (1Cor 15:30-32). This meant that, even though he was already dead in Christ, he had to choose every day to get rid of pride and humble himself and die to his desires and feelings and be willing to suffer for Christ and live as a witness for Him.

Thus, losing your life for Christ is not just a one time decision but also a path that you walk where Christ is your life. Whenever you die to self by obeying God or yielding to the Holy Spirit or doing what is right, this is denying self and carrying your cross. When you do this, self becomes less and the life of God in you becomes more powerful so that you are conformed more and more into the image of Christ (Rom 5:4-5, 8:29, 2Cor 3:18, Col 3:10). This is how you find your life.

Each day and each moment you have to decide to deny self, carry your cross, and follow Jesus. This is losing your life for Christ. You deny self by getting rid of pride, humbling yourself, laying down what you want, putting God first, and having the heart of a servant for serving God and helping others (Matt 20:25-28, John 13:12-17, Phi 2:3-8). You carry your cross by surrendering to God, obeying God, and doing the will of God no matter what the cost is (Matt 10:22, Luke 6:46-49, 8:21, 11:28, Rom 8:17, 12:1-2, 2Tim 3:12). You follow Jesus by making Him your Lord, loving Him, and seeking and wanting to know God (Mark 12:29-31, Luke 6:40, John 14:15,21,23-24, 1John 2:3-6). When you deny self and carry your cross and follow Jesus, this is losing sight of yourself and seeing Christ as your life.

Losing your life for Christ is both what has already happened and a process that you work out. This is because the new life is both a present possession and a goal to pursue and it is both a work of God and a work by you (Rom 6:4-18, Gal 5:16-25, Eph 4:22-24, Phi 2:12-13). You have already died to self, but you also have to work to keep self dead.

How do you die to self? You have to make self less and Christ greater in your heart and life. John the Baptist said about Jesus, "He must become greater; I must become less" (John 3:30, NIV). You then have to make an effort to cleanse yourself and your life from everything that is unholy and anything that is an idol between you and God. Paul exhorted his associate Timothy,

"[19]Nevertheless, God's solid foundation stands firm, sealed with this inscription: 'The Lord knows those who are his,' and, 'Everyone who confesses the name of the Lord must turn away from wickedness.' [20]In a large house there are articles not only of gold and silver, but also of wood and clay; some are for noble purposes and some for ignoble. [21]If a man cleanses himself from the latter, he will be an instrument for noble purposes, made holy, useful to the Master and prepared to do any good work. [22]Flee the evil desires of youth, and pursue righteousness, faith, love and peace, along with those who call on the Lord out of a pure heart" (2Tim 2:19-22, NIV; cf. 1Cor 6:12, 10:23, Heb 12:1, 1John 5:21; Num 16:5).

As you cleanse yourself and your life from pride and the weights and bonds that drag you down and from what is unclean, impure, not honorable, not beneficial, and not edifying (not building you up) and you strive to put God first, God will do a work in your heart and life. When this happens, the life of God will become stronger in you and you will be conformed more into the image of Christ and more anointed in the Holy Spirit.

It is your decision each day whether to live for Christ or to live for yourself. Each day you must choose to either walk in the Spirit or walk in the flesh. Each day you must choose how you will think and how you will act and what voice you will listen to. Each day you must choose to seek God and desire to know Him. Each day you must put down pride and humble yourself. Each day you must choose to die to self and lose your life for Christ, but this can only be done if you see dying to self and losing your life for Christ as a joyous celebration that brings freedom and blessing.

Christ found joy in dying to self and going to the cross. Even though Christ despised the cross, the Bible says that Jesus "for the joy set before him endured the cross" (Heb 12:2). It was the joy of doing the greatest work in history, the joy of helping the most people, the joy of defeating Satan and the kingdom of darkness, and the joy of seeing Himself with God the Father. Jesus was able to endure the cross because of the joy set before Him.

You should also be motivated to die to self and lose your life for Christ and to live for Christ when you see the love of Christ for you. The Bible says,

"[14]For the love of Christ controls us, having concluded this, that one died for all, therefore all died; [15]and He died for all, that they who live should no longer live for themselves, but for Him who died and rose again on their behalf" (2Cor 5:14-15, NASB).[12]

Thus, when you see the love of Christ, that He died for your sins on the cross to give you eternal life with God, this love should have such a hold on you that you are compelled to die to self and lose your life for Christ and live completely for Him. When you see the love of Christ for you (when you received Christ), this should compel you to no longer live for self but to live for Christ.

It is dying to self and losing your life for Christ that is the key to being transformed into the image of Christ and doing the will of God. God can only use you in proportion to how much you are dying to self and losing your life for Christ (and this includes repentance). This is the person God can use for His glory. You can be doing a lot of activity for God, but whether you are doing the will of God depends upon how much you have died to self and are losing your life for Christ. It does not matter how gifted or anointed you are (or think you are), you will only be like Christ and do the will of God according to how much you have died to self and are losing your life for Christ.

---

12- The Greek verb that is translated as "controls" is *sunecho* (SC-#4912, also spelled *synecho*), which means "to hold together, press together, take hold, hold fast, constrain, control, compel" (Luke 4:38, 8:37,45, 19:43, Acts 18:5, 2Cor 5:14, Phi 1:23). This word is the intensive form of *echo* (has/have) and signifies that something has a strong hold or influence on you.

This is the pathway to the anointing and power of God. It is dying to self and losing your life for Christ that births and increases the miracle power of God in you, not having boldness or seeing oneself as a king. You may yearn to have the power of the resurrection of Christ in your life like Paul did, but it is only by dying to self and losing your life for Christ that the miracle power of God will be manifested through you. This is the testimony of all who are really anointed in the gifts of the Holy Spirit.

This is the pathway to receiving blessing and favor from God. God favors and pours out His blessings upon the one who is losing his or her life for Christ. The hyper blessing message that you hear preached is really for the one who is dying to self and losing one's life for Christ (although this is never mentioned). God blesses you in proportion to how much you have died to self and are losing your life for Christ, not how much faith you have to get things.

Finally, there are four passages of Scripture that can help you focus on losing your life for Christ and pursuing the will and purposes of God for your life.

"[19]Do not lay up for yourselves treasures on earth, where moth and rust destroy and where thieves break in and steal; [20]but lay up for yourselves treasures in heaven, where neither moth nor rust destroys and where thieves do not break in and steal. [21]For where your treasure is, there your heart will be also....[24]No one can serve two masters; for either he will hate the one and love the other, or else he will be loyal to the one and despise the other. You cannot serve God and mammon. [25]Therefore I say to you, do not worry about your life, what you will drink; nor about your body, what you will put on. Is not life more than food and the body more than clothing?...[33]But seek first the kingdom of God and His righteousness, and all these things shall be added unto you" (Matt 6:19-21,24-25,33, NKJV).

"[1]Since, then, you have been raised with Christ, set your hearts on things above, where Christ is seated at the right hand of God. [2]Set your minds on things above, not on earthly things. [3]For you died, and your life is now hidden with Christ in God. [4]When Christ, who is your life, appears, then you also will appear with him in glory" (Col 3:1-4, NIV; Matt 13:18-23, Luke 8:11-15).

"[15]Do not love the world or anything in the world. If anyone loves the world, the love of the Father is not in him. [16]For everything in the world- the cravings of sinful man, the lust of his eyes and the boasting of what he has and does- comes not from the Father but from the world. [17]The world and its desires pass away, but the one who does the will of God lives forever" (1John 2:15-17, NIV).

"[16]Therefore we do not lose heart. Though outwardly we are wasting away, yet inwardly we are being renewed day by day. [17]For our light and momentary troubles are achieving or us an eternal glory that far outweighs them all. [18]So we fix our eyes not on what is seen, but on what is unseen. For what is seen is temporary, but what is unseen is eternal" (2Cor 4:16-18, NIV).

You must set before yourself the kingdom of God and Christ (who is the way into the kingdom of God). Your treasure is either the kingdom of God (the rule of God) or this world, it is either Christ or the possessions of this world, and where your treasure is, this is where your heart will be. Is your heart with Christ and the kingdom of God or is it with this world and its ways and possessions? This world is just temporary, but the kingdom of God is eternal. Therefore, store up for yourself treasures in heaven, investing as much as possible of your time, efforts, possessions, and money in what is eternal.

When your treasure is the kingdom of God and Christ, your first concern is for the kingdom of God (how to live in this kingdom and build this kingdom), and you are not consumed with the things of this world. If your primary concern is with the things of this world, you will be consumed with the worries and pleasures of life and lose sight of the kingdom of God and Christ. Therefore, set your heart upon Christ and the kingdom of God, not this world and the things of this world. While we must work to meet our needs and be diligent about the practical things of life, we cannot be consumed with or fall in love with these things but we must trust God and put God first. If you take care of the things of God, God will take care of your life. Therefore, make your first priority to seek God and to know Him (His presence, will, and revelation) and God promises that He will take care of your life.

Seek first the kingdom of God and His righteousness and have your heart and mind set on spiritual things and what has eternal significance. Make God the most important thing in your life and make Him first. Determine to obey God and to pursue His will and purposes. This is what your heart must be set upon, but your heart will only be set upon these things by dying to self and losing your life for Christ and making a commitment to live for Jesus. This must be your focus, your foundational purpose in life. When you die to self and lose your life for Christ and live for Him, the life of God will be working in you and you will find purpose and fulfillment and hope for the future.

Finally, I wish to end this study with the prayer of Saint Francis of Assisi, a monk who devoted his life to unconditional love and selfless service. This prayer has tremendous insight for what it means to die to self and to live for Christ.

Lord, make me an instrument of Thy peace.
Where there is hatred, let me sow love.
Where there is injury, pardon.
Where there is doubt, faith.
Where there is despair, hope.
Where there is darkness, light.
Where there is sadness, joy.

O divine Master, grant to me
that I may not seek to be consoled, but to console,
that I may not seek to be understood, but to understand,
that I may not seek to be loved, but to love.
For it is in giving that we receive;
It is in forgiving that we are forgiven;
And it is in dying to self that we are born to eternal life.

## Summary: The Search for Purpose

A. Defining purpose: Purpose can ask why I am here on earth, but purpose is the how of life. How will I fulfill and find that which gives me meaning?
1. Purpose is what you do, who you relate to, and how you spend your time. Purpose is having a goal and working and persevering toward attaining or accomplishing this goal.
2. There is general purpose. We find purpose through fulfilling work, meaningful relationships, and self improvement. This is the search for achievement, love, and maturity.
3. There is foundational purpose. Your foundational purpose is your central mission in life and sets your heart and attitude for fulfilling your purpose in life.

B. How you find purpose:
1. In order to give yourself to a cause and to live for someone, you must die to self and lose your life for that person and cause. Will you die to self unto God and lose your life for Christ?
2. If you want to know Christ and the power of His resurrection and be transformed into the image of Christ and walk in the Spirit, you must lose your life for Christ. Losing your life for Christ is dying to self (as Christ died to self at the cross) and doing the will of God. It is denying self (losing sight of self), carrying your cross (obeying God), and following Jesus (making Jesus Lord).

C. How you lose your life for Christ
1. It is a work of God.
2. See losing your life for Christ as a joyous celebration and a pathway to freedom.
3. It is a decision you have to make every day, but be motivated by the joy set before you and the love of Christ for you.
4. Get the Word of God into your heart (Matt 6:19-34, Rom 6:3-23, Gal 2:20, Col 3:1-4, 1John 2:15-17, 2Cor 4:16-18).

Chapter 4

# The Search for Achievement

We have a need for achievement.[1] We are created in the image of God, and God created us to achieve. God himself achieved great things when He created the heavens and the earth and all living creatures, and this desire to achieve great things has been placed in us. Thus, we have a natural desire for greatness, a desire to do something important, a desire to feel that we have made a lasting impact in this world, that my life counts and I am needed and appreciated. The desire for achievement also includes a desire to create, a desire to discover, and a desire for beauty. The desire for achievement, of course, must be balanced by the belief that God Almighty is Creator and Lord, otherwise, we can become proud and destructive, but God has created us to achieve great things.

The way we achieve things is through work. Work is defined as any activity of the body or mind. Work can involve manual labor, a mental process, or doing both together. Work can be producing, creating, designing, discovering, planning, buying, investing, building, repairing, operating, managing, computing, performing, teaching, speaking, writing, or thinking. Work is engaging in any activity or task that is doing something useful. It is through work that we find achievement, and having fulfilling work

---

1- It was difficult choosing a title for this chapter because no word seemed sufficient. There were several choices that were considered: the search for work (the working title, but too mundane), the search for ministry (left out secular vocation), the search for work and ministry (wanted to have just one word), the search for service (but we might not search for this), the search for vocation (sounded too narrow), the search for activity (sounded too general), the search for success (sounded good but not specific enough), the search for accomplishment (sounded good but not good enough, but it led to achievement). The search for achievement was chosen because it is what we are really searching for and a major reason why we can enjoy work.

is one of the three ways that we find purpose in life. Thus, this chapter is as much about work as it is about achievement. We must work in order to achieve things, and we must find fulfilling work in order to find purpose.

It is good for a man and a woman to work. When God created man and woman, He gave them dominion over the earth and all living creatures, and it was their role to manage the earth (Gen 1:26-30, 2:15, Psalm 8:5, 115:16). Man and woman were commissioned by God to oversee all living creatures and to work the earth, tilling the soil and taming the animals for food and harvesting the ground and mining the earth for the necessities and luxuries of life. They were to be good stewards of what God had entrusted to them. Thus, God ordained man and woman to work. God himself worked to create the heavens and the earth (Gen 2:1-2). God meant for work to be enjoyable, fulfilling, profitable, and the means for finding achievement and a measure of purpose.

Since God ordained work and intended it to be fulfilling and the means for finding achievement and purpose, we have a need for work. However, when man and woman fell into sin, work and life changed. Life and work became difficult. Work was not as fulfilling and achievement was not as easy and forthcoming. Thus, many people do not like work and do not want to work and try to get out of work, but we still have a natural desire to engage in fulfilling work that will bring us achievement and give us a measure of purpose.

Even if there is not a conscious desire to work, there is still an innate desire in each one of us to have fulfilling work that gives us purpose and enables us to achieve. If you are not finding work and not achieving anything significant in life, you will battle emptiness and discouragement every day of your life. You may not understand why you feel this way, but it is because God created you for work and achievement. God created you to do work that will utilize your gifts, abilities, and motivations. God created you to do useful and fulfilling labor and activities that will enable you to be successful, fulfill your dreams, do the will of God, have purpose, and achieve good things and even great things.

Jesus Christ talked about the importance of work. He said that He was always doing the Father's work and exhorted us to be fruitful in good works, even admonishing those who were lazy.

"My food is to do the will of Him [Father God] who sent Me, and to finish His work" (John 4:34, NKJV; cf. John 5:17,19, 9:4, 17:4).

"Let your light so shine before men, that they may see your good works and glorify your Father who is in heaven" (Matt 5:16, NKJV; cf. Matt 9:37-38 & Prov 10:5, Matt 25:16-18, 25:31-46, Luke 19:12-19, John 4:35-38, 1Cor 15:58, Gal 6:9-10, Eph 2:10, Col 1:10, 1Tim 6:17-19, Titus 3:8,14, Rev 2:2).

"[24]Then he who had received the one talent came and said, 'Master, I knew you to be a hard man, reaping where you have not sown, and gathering where you have not scattered seed. [25]And I was afraid, and went and hid your talent in the ground. Look, there you have what is yours'. [26]But his master answered and said to him, 'You wicked and slothful servant, you knew that I reap where I did not sow, and gather where I have not scattered seed. [27]Therefore you ought to have put my money with the bankers, and then at my coming I would have received back my own with interest. [28]Therefore take the talent from him, and give it to him who has ten talents. [29]For to everyone who has, more will be given, and he will have abundance; but from him who does not have will be taken away even what he has. [30]And cast the unprofitable servant into the outer darkness. There will be weeping and gnashing of teeth'" (Matt 25:24-30, NKJV, see 25:14-30; cf. Luke 19:11-27).

God wants us to be diligent about working and to be rich in good deeds by using our talents (gifts, abilities, creativity). It is those who do work who will achieve good things and do the will of God to help others and build the kingdom of God. Thus, these are the ones who deserve to be given more, for they will do more with what they receive. Those who refuse to work do not deserve to receive more and will be punished for being slothful and useless.

When discussing the issue of work, there is also the issue of time. We should understand that one day we will die. Our time on this earth is not forever; it is temporary with only a certain number of minutes, hours, days, and years to live. Even if we do not comprehend this, we have a natural desire to make our time in this world count. This is a deep seated desire. And as you see the days marching onward and see your parent's generation dying off and then your generation dying off, you realize more and more that your time on this earth is only temporary. Time then becomes a factor that pushes you to try to use your time wisely so that you will find achievement and fulfillment before you die.

Thus, we have a need to spend our time engaging in useful and significant activities and to enjoy life. You want your days to count, not to count the days. You have to spend your time doing something with your life and doing things that are useful and significant and enjoyable, otherwise, you will not see any purpose in life. You must be doing something constructive with your time, and while there should be time for enjoyment, most of your time should be spent doing something that is useful or significant. Those who are satisfied in just watching television or videos or surfing the internet or talking on the phone and then eating and sleeping are people who need to get a life and learn to do something useful and constructive. Make yourself useful, not useless, and make your time on this earth count.

## Section 4B: The Domains of Work

There are three basic domains of work. There is vocational work (which includes being a homemaker or student). This is where you receive monetary compensation (breadwinner) or you pursue education or training that will hopefully lead to monetary compensation (student) or you contribute to the welfare of a household and the care of children without getting paid (homemaker), and it must be said that the most important work is the care and nurture of children. There is volunteer service (work done in the secular realm where you are not paid). There is ministry (work done in or through a church or religious organization where you are not paid). Every follower of Jesus Christ is called to ministry, although there is also vocational ministry where you receive monetary compensation for ministry, and some people work in full time vocational ministry (Acts 13:2, 14:26). It is very important to work and to be useful, whether it is working for pay or being a homemaker or getting an education or doing volunteer work or serving in ministry. This is being useful

90

and using your time wisely, and it strengthens the family, the community, and yourself.

These three domains of work will now be examined individually. We are called to ministry, vocational work, and volunteer service.

## The Call to Ministry

If you are a follower of Jesus Christ, you are called to ministry. You are called to serve God and to be a minister to others. We serve God and minister to others by following Jesus and the righteousness of God, helping others, and building the kingdom of God (Matt 20:25-28, 22:39, 28:18-20, John 13:13-17, Gal 5:13-14, 6:10, Eph 2:10, Phi 2:3-8). Building the kingdom of God is growing spiritually yourself, bringing people into the kingdom, building people up, and living by kingdom principles. Concerning ministry and spiritual gifts, the apostle Peter says,

"[10]As each has received a gift, minister it to one another, as good stewards of the manifold grace of God. [11]If anyone speaks, let him speak as the oracles [words] of God. If anyone ministers, let him do it as with the ability which God supplies, that in all things God may be glorified through Jesus Christ, to whom belong the glory and the dominion forever and ever. Amen" (1Pet 4:10-11, NKJV; cf. Rom 1:11, Heb 2:4).

Everyone who is born of the Spirit has been called to ministry and has received at least one spiritual gift for ministry. Spiritual gifts are imparted into you by the Holy Spirit and activated through surrender and obedience to God. The Greek word translated here as "gift" is *charisma*.[2] It is a gift that comes by the grace of God, grace being a gift of God's ability and position. You speak "the words" that are in your heart from God and you serve "with the ability which God supplies."

---

2- The Greek word *charisma* (SC#-5486, noun) literally means "grace-gift" (Rom 1:11, 6:23, 12:6, 1Cor 12:4,9,28,30,31, 1Tim 4:14, 2Tim 1:6, 1Pet 4:10). It is derived from *charis*, which is the word for "grace" (SC-#5485). The plural form is *charismata*. It is interesting to note that salvation, the greatest gift of all, is called a *charisma* (Rom 5:15,16, 6:23).

We are exhorted to minister our gifts to others, and as we do this we will be "good stewards of the manifold grace of God". Thus, we receive spiritual gifts by the grace of God and using your spiritual gifts will make you a good steward of the grace God has given you. The primary purpose of spiritual gifts is "that in all things God may be glorified through Jesus Christ." When you minister by the Holy Spirit, people are helped and can sense that God is real and at work, and when this happens, God is glorified.

In this passage in First Peter we are exhorted twice to "minister" to one another. It says: "As each one has received a gift, minister it to one another" and "If anyone ministers, let him do it as with the ability which God supplies". Thus, it can be said that every follower of Jesus Christ is a minister. We have come to use the term "minister" to refer to someone who has an official position in a church or is in full time ministry, but this is not how the Bible uses this word.

The Greek word translated as "minister" in this passage is *diakoneo*, which means "to serve". This word was used to signify the rendering of any kind of service and is translated as "serve" or "minister". The corresponding noun is *diakonia*, which is translated as "servant" or "minister" and was the standard term for signifying a servant. The other corresponding noun, denoting the service, is *diakonos*, which is translated as "service" or "ministry". Thus, to minister is to serve, and to serve is to minister. When we serve others, we minister to them, and whenever we are a servant to others, we are being a minister to them, and any service for God that we render is a ministry.[3]

Thus, everyone who is born of the Spirit has been called to spiritual ministry. This means that every follower of Jesus Christ is a priest of God. A priest is someone who offers worship to God and ministers to others by interceding with God on their behalf. This is the doctrine of the priesthood of the believer, and this doctrine is clearly stated in First Peter.

---

3- *Diakoneo* (SC#-1247, verb) literally means "to wait on tables" and is translated as "to serve, to minister" (Matt 8:15, 20:28, 25:44, 27:55, John 12:26, Acts 6:2). *Diakonia* (SC-#1248, noun) means "servant, minister" (Matt 20:26, Mark 10:43, Rom 13:4, 16:1). *Diakonos* (SC-#1249, noun) means "service, ministry" (Acts 6:1, 1Cor 12:5, 2Cor 5:18, 8:4, Eph 4:12, Heb 1:14).

"4Coming to Him as to a living stone, rejected indeed by men, but chosen by God and precious, 5you also, as living stones, are being built up a spiritual house, a holy priesthood, to offer up spiritual sacrifices acceptable to God through Jesus Christ" (1Pet 2:4-5, NKJV; 1Pet 2:9- "a royal priesthood").

God has made us "a holy priesthood" and "a royal priesthood" and calls us a kingdom of priests (Rev 1:6, 5:10, 20:6; Isa 61:6). Therefore, every disciple of Christ (clergy and laity, elder and youth, male and female) is a priest unto God and able "to offer up spiritual sacrifices acceptable to God through Jesus Christ" (2:5b).

The foundation for being ministers and priests of God and receiving spiritual gifts is found in Galatians 3:26-29.

(Gal 3:26-29)- "26You are all sons of God through faith in Christ Jesus, 27for all of you who were baptized into Christ have clothed yourselves with Christ. 28There is neither Jew nor Greek, slave nor free, male nor female, for you are all one in Christ Jesus. 29If you belong to Christ, then you are Abraham's seed, and heirs according to the promise" (NIV; see Gal 3:2,14, 4:4-7; cf. Rom 10:12, 1Cor 12:13, Gal 5:6, 6:15, Col 3:11; the promise- Luke 24:49, Acts 1:4-8, 2:17-18,38-39).

Spiritual gifts (Eph 4:7,8,11, Rom 12:6-8, 1Cor 12:7-11) are available to every believer according to the grace of God. Through faith in Christ we are "sons of God" who have been clothed with Christ and made heirs of the Holy Spirit, and it is through the Holy Spirit that we receive spiritual gifts. Thus, God sees us clothed with Christ and freely pours out the Spirit upon all. The spiritual gifts are imparted by the Holy Spirit, so it is only through the Holy Spirit that we are anointed in spiritual gifts, ministry, and leadership in the kingdom of God. Who we are in the body only determines the personality and perspective of these gifts. In Christ there is no race or nationality, there is no position or rank, there is no gender. Spiritual gifts are given freely to each one through the Holy Spirit without regard to one's place in the natural realm.

Even the ascension gifts of Christ (Eph 4:11) are spiritual gifts given by the grace of God and imparted by the Holy Spirit. They are not governmental offices (overseer, elder, deacon) or positions instituted by man. The ascension gifts of Christ are spiritual gifts that are freely given regardless of our race, position, gender, or whoever we might be in the natural realm (Gal 3:28, 1Cor 12:13, Col 3:11). God calls ascension gift ministers (apostles, prophets, evangelists, pastors, teachers) from both men and women,[4] from every rank in life, from every people group, and from every type of person. So do not look at who you are in the natural, for who you are right now may seem contrary to the gift that God has for you, but see yourself clothed in Christ and anointed with the Holy Spirit and let God reveal your spiritual gifts to you.

People have a tendency to look for a king, someone who acts and looks like a king and will do ministry for them, but God wants us to stop looking for a king. There is no king except for Jesus Christ. While God has appointed spiritual leaders in the Church, one role of these leaders is "for the perfecting of the saints into a work of ministry, unto the building up of the body of Christ" (Eph 4:12, NASB). Thus, God calls every believer into the ministry of God, and it absolutely requires the ministry of every believer in order to achieve the complete spiritual growth and full maturity of the body of Christ (Eph 4:13-16, Col 2:19).

God does not look at the outward appearance as man does (1Sam 16:7-8), but He looks for people who have a heart for Him. God looks for those who are surrendered to Him and love Him and are motivated to help others and build the kingdom of God and bring glory to Him. These are the people God chooses. God chooses and anoints those who have a heart for Him and will obey Him, not those who have great abilities and talents. Thus, God does not choose the qualified, but He qualifies those He chooses,

---

4- The Holy Spirit is poured out freely upon all who are "sons of God" through faith in Christ Jesus. The spiritual gifts, including the ascension gifts of Christ, are bestowed by the grace of God through the Holy Spirit and are imparted to our spirit, and are given without regard to who we are in the natural realm. Thus, it must be understood that women can receive any spiritual gift, even an ascension gift and the gift of managing (Rom 12:8). The Scriptures affirm that a woman is able to preach the word of God and prophesy and can be a spiritual leader and anointed in the Holy Spirit (Exod 4:24-26, 15:20-21, Judges 4:4-10, 2Sam 20:15-22, 2Chr 34:22-28, 2Kngs 22:14-20, Micah 6:4, Matt 28:18-20, Mark 16:15-18, Luke 1:41-42,46-55, 2:36-38, 8:1-3, Acts 2:17-18, 18:24-26, 21:8-9, Rom 12:6-8, 15:14, 16:1-7,12-13, 1Cor 11:5, 12:7-11, 14:26, Gal 3:26-29, Eph 4:7,11-16, Phi 4:2-3, Col 3:16, 4:15, Titus 2:3).

equipping and anointing those He calls. Therefore, find your gifts and ministry and work to build the body of Christ and the kingdom of God, and remember that your greatest ministry is to your immediate family. If you do this, you will do the will of God and fulfill your calling and destiny in God.[5]

If you forsake your calling to serve God, you will experience emptiness and a lack of fulfillment, and, in time, if you continue down this road, you will become miserable. A friend of mine was talking with her father during his last days as he was dying. She said that he confessed to her that, although he had been successful in business, he now realized he had forsaken the calling of God on his life. Moreover, he now could see that this rejection of the calling of God had caused much pain to build up in his heart, and this pain had been the root of his drinking problem and his anger and the physical and emotional abuse that he had given his family over the years. If you are not doing what God has called you to do, emptiness and pain will build up in your heart and produce a bitter root that will adversely affect your life and the lives of everyone around you. You must serve God if you want emotional wholeness.

**The Call to Vocation and Work**

It is important to work and have a vocation, and it is important to do work that either earns monetary compensation or contributes to the welfare of a household. There has been a search for work in recent years during this persistent economic recession, and even when the economy has seemed to pick up, it still has been difficult to find work and good paying jobs.

There is great distress when you cannot find a job and do not have the money to pay the bills and support yourself and a family. It is very difficult to think of anything else, including helping others or serving God, when you do not know how you will

---

5- For understanding the spiritual gifts, see *The Spiritual Gifts (Part 1): The Ascension Gifts of Christ and the Functional Gifts of God* and *The Spiritual Gifts (Part 2): The Gifts of the Holy Spirit* by Tim Williams. For understanding the role of women in ministry, see *The Reconciliation of 1Timothy 2:11-15 with Galatians 3:26-28 in the Context of Women in Ministry: An Eschatological Tension* by Tim Williams. For understanding your calling in God, see *The Battle to Fulfill your Destiny in God* by Juanita Folsom and Tim Williams.

provide for your needs. Even when you have faith that God will supply your needs or lead you to that needed source of income (Matt 6:25-34), it is a difficult place to be in to live day after day without knowing how your needs will be met. It is also a difficult place to be in if you have to rely upon charity to support yourself.

Work gives us dignity, especially for men, and earning money gives us self esteem as well as fulfillment. Working and supporting yourself (and your family) contributes a lot to one's self esteem. On the other hand, even though we should give to the poor, receiving charity over a certain period of time will erode your self esteem, and, moreover, not doing something useful with your time for an extended season will erode your character.

Work that earns money is a very practical thing. You need money to live. It has been said that the practical things in life are spiritual things (because they are important), and I believe this is true. Books on the spiritual life that talk about work or purpose never talk about vocational work, but having work that earns sufficient income is very important and having a good paying job and a good career is very beneficial.

The Bible talks a lot about work and money, especially being a good steward of your money and the importance of working. I believe that churches can do more in helping people find jobs and careers, although I see that many churches that serve the poor have programs to help people find jobs and careers. A church gains a lot when its people have good jobs and are earning good money.

The apostle Paul believed very strongly in working and having a vocation that would support oneself and enable you to give. Paul was a good role model for being a worker and had some enlightening things to say about work. Paul says,

"[33]I have coveted no one's silver or gold or apparel. [34]Yes, you yourselves know that these hands have provided for my necessities, and for those who were with me. [35]I have shown you in every way, by laboring like this, that you must support the weak. And remember the words of the Lord Jesus, that He said, 'It is more blessed to give than to receive'" (Acts 20:33-35, NKJV).

"Let no one who stole steal no longer, but rather let him labor, working with his hands what is good, that he may have something to give him who has need" (Eph 4:28, NKJV).

"Our people must learn to devote themselves to doing what is good, in order that they may provide for daily necessities and not live unproductive lives" (Titus 3:14, NIV; cf. Titus 3:8).

"[11]Make it your ambition to lead a quiet life, to mind your own business and to work with your hands, just as we told you, [12]so that your daily life may win the respect of outsiders and so that you will not be dependent on anybody" (1Thes 4:11-12, NIV; cf. 5:14).

"[6]In the name of the Lord Jesus, we command you brothers, to keep away from every brother who is idle and does not live according to the teaching you received from us. [7]For you yourselves know how you ought to follow our example. We were not idle when we were with you, [8]nor did we eat anyone's food without paying for it. On the contrary, we worked day and night, laboring and toiling so that we would not be a burden to any of you. [9]We did this, not because we do not have the right to such help, but in order to make ourselves a model for you to follow. [10]For even when we were with you, we gave you this rule: 'If a man will not work, he shall not eat'. [11]We hear that some among you are idle. They are not busy; they are busybodies. [12]Such people we command and urge in the Lord Jesus Christ to settle down and earn the bread they eat" (2Thes 3:6-12, NIV; cf. Matt 25:24-30, Prov 10.5, 12:11, 14:23, 18:9, 20:4,13, 21:25, Eccl 9:10, 10:18).

It is apparent from these passages that Paul believed very strongly in working to support oneself, and set himself as a role model for this practice even though he was entitled to receive offerings from his churches. Paul was in full time ministry as much as anyone else, but he still worked at a trade to take care of himself and his ministry expenses (Acts 20:33-35, 28:30, 1Cor 4:11-12, 9:3-6,11-12, 2Cor 11:7-9, 1Thes 2:9, 2Thes 3:7-9).

Paul had a trade, a secular vocation, and it was making tents (Paul the tentmaker, see Acts 18:1-4). In those days it was traditional for Rabbis (and Paul had been trained as a Rabbi, Phi

3:5) to learn a trade because it was not considered to be honorable to accept money for teaching the word of God (although this may not have been practiced by every Rabbi). It was by making and selling tents that Paul was able to support himself and his helpers without asking for offerings, although at times he was given unsolicited gifts (Phi 4:10-20, 2Cor 11:7-9).

Paul apparently wanted to be an example for being industrious and to show that work was important (Acts 20:35, 2Cor 11:9, 2Thes 3:9). He also did not want anyone to be able to accuse him of being in the ministry for the money (1Cor 9:11-12, 2Cor 2:17, 4:2; cf. Acts 13:6-12, 16:16-19, 19:19,23-28). While there is nothing wrong in receiving money for doing ministry and those in full time ministry should receive their livelihood from tithes and offerings (Matt 10:5-10, Mark 6:8-10, Luke 10:1-9, 1Cor 9:1-18, Gal 6:6, 1Tim 5:17-18; Num 18:21,24), Paul's practice can offer us much insight and wisdom about the importance of work.

Paul's attitude and practice concerning work is different than what is seen today. I have seen people who fancy themselves as leaders and believe they have a leadership ministry gift (and maybe they do), and they desire so much to have a paid position in a church or ministry. This desire may be such that they will not work a regular job while they are hoping and waiting for a paid position to open up. There are also others who have such a deep desire for God that they lose sight of the importance of having a livelihood to support oneself. They flounder here and there and do not do what they need to do to have a job that will support them. Both types of people end up being a burden to others and their church.

It is true that you can become so heavenly minded that you are no earthly good. You may not agree with this saying, but it is true. You can be so set on what you think is spiritual that you are not diligent about the practical things of life, but the practical things of life are very important. When one is not diligent about the practical things of life so that it places a burden on others or one is not able to give to the Lord and help others, then it can be said that you are being so heavenly minded that you are no earthly good.

Paul had this problem with the Thessalonians. It is apparent that many people in this church were quitting their jobs (1Thes 2:3-5,9, 4:11-12, 5:14a, 2Thes 3:6-12), maybe because they believed that the return of Christ was very near (1Thes 1:10, 2:19,

3:13, 4:13-18, 5:1-6,23, 2Thes 1:5-10, 2:1-12). Paul had to exhort these believers not to practice an escapist lifestyle but to live a regular life, for at least one thing can be said- somebody has to pay the bills. You cannot allow a heart for ministry or a yearning for the Lord to cause you to lose sight of the importance of working so that you can support yourself and a family, give to the work of the Lord, give to those in need, and not be a burden to others.

We must also realize that, if the kingdom of God is to reach every area of society, God must have His people enter every area of society. There is a time to be alone with God, and there is a time to reach out to your community. A good way for you to reach out to your community is being in the workplace. This is called being a "tentmaker" (because Paul was a tentmaker).

I have seen how this has worked in my own life. When I was offered a job as a counselor at a juvenile residential facility (a fancy name for a boys prison), I did not want to do it, but I felt that this is what God wanted me to do, and so I accepted the position. During my time there I saw how those boys were able to experience the kingdom of God through myself and other workers. They believed that I cared about them and saw me as a good man. I always challenged them to become a better person and make the necessary changes so that they would not go back to crime. I also encouraged them to seek God and gave a Bible (from donations) to those who wanted one. A good portion of those boys made a decision to leave crime and live a good life, with some seeking God through reading the Bible and praying and going to church. Some made a decision to receive Christ into their hearts (through local ministries or their own devotional time), and this is how most of these guys really changed (it was not the therapy program).

I always felt that we had a positive influence on those boys, and this experience showed me that if we want to change the world in a positive way, especially for Christ, we have to get into the world. Thus, not only is work important in itself, but being in the workplace gets you out into the world so that the world can experience the salt and the light of the kingdom of God and the gospel of Jesus Christ.

Another way to bring the gospel and the kingdom of God into the world is having a business that is also a ministry. For example, the Seventh Day Adventist Church has developed a major hospital network in the state of Florida (the Florida Hospital system). These hospitals have the finest doctors, medical staff, and technology, and some have been highly rated by consumer organizations. These hospitals provide good jobs for the community, they provide a valuable service for helping people, they provide excellent care, and they provide a setting where people can receive medical care in a godly and Christ honoring environment. The staff truly cares for you and is willing to pray with you and talk about spiritual things. This is work that helps people in a wonderful way, brings much glory to God, and helps build the kingdom of God.

Work is not only important for helping people, but it is also important for earning money. Work is how you earn money to support yourself and a family, help others, and support the work of God. It has been said that it takes money to build the kingdom of God, and this is true. It takes money to do things. Money is important and it gives you opportunity for doing more things. Therefore, make money your friend; just don't fall in love with money (Matt 6:24, 1Tim 6:10). Make money your friend and learn to invest money, and most of all, learn to invest your money and possessions in the kingdom of God (Matt 6:19-24, 1Tim 6:17-19).

It is good to have a good job and a good career (and this could be just having steady work). Even if you plan to be a homemaker, it is good to have a vocation that you can fall back on during times of waiting or difficulty. In order to have a good job or career today, you may have to get education or training for an occupation. It is becoming more and more difficult today to find a good paying job without having some kind of degree or certification. And when the construction industry is doing poorly, as it has been for the last few years, it is very difficult for a lot of men and teenage boys to find work. You might find a good career in sales or management if you are willing to work hard. You could also start your own business if you have the vision and ability for this, but this takes a lot of wisdom and hard work. If this is your dream, however, God can give you ideas and plans for a business or investment if He knows you will give this business or investment to Him. You have to be diligent to find a good job and career, and it might take more time than you want to find that right job or career or have that steady income. Thus, it is important to have perseverance and faith in God and even faith in yourself when looking for a job or career.

I do not believe that America is as blessed as it used to be, although financial blessing will come to those who work hard. When a nation is blessed, blessing overflows into all parts of society. This used to be true for America, but not now, and this is because people are in love with this world and are not following God. Moreover, we live in an increasingly socialistic society where the government tries to be God, and more and more people like it this way. Socialism does not create wealth but breeds poverty. Socialism will not get you out of economic hardship but will get you into economic depression. You cannot have an increasing number of people living off the government and expect to have a healthy economy, and neither can you have increasing taxes and government regulation and expect prosperity. Socialism leads to a downward spiral for an economy. Wealth is created by business and the free enterprise system, not government programs or printing more money. Therefore, government must be responsible to provide a healthy business environment.[6] The most important thing for a society and what will help it socially more than anything else, besides its people following God, is having a strong economy with plenty of good paying jobs.[7]

I have been trained in career counseling and have had a lot of experience looking for employment and have even taught a class in church on finding a job and career. The practical principals that I teach are: 1) work hard at looking for a job, 2) tell people that you need a job, 3) go to your local career center and make use of their resources for finding a job and career and learning job seeking skills, 4) get the education or training that will help you get a good job and career, 5) make yourself useful while you are looking for a job (e.g., doing volunteer work, which lets people know you are willing to work, and this can lead to a job), and 6) maintain a positive mental attitude and believe in yourself.

---

6- And even though greed in the financial markets was the cause of the recent economic recession, it was the socialistic program of the government in the mortgage industry that created the pathway for this greed. When the government pushed for more liberal loans and guaranteed these loans without proper oversight, this opened the door for financial institutions to offer unsafe loans.

7- This idea was reinforced by my multicultural counseling professor, a middle-aged black woman. She said that the best way to promote racial harmony was to have a strong economy with plenty of good paying jobs.

There are also scriptural principles that I teach for finding a job and career. First, believe that God wants to meet your needs and will show you the supply for these needs (Matt 6:25-34, Phi 4:19). You can claim to have your basic needs supplied. Second, ask God for a job and step out in faith to look for a job, and, moreover, seek the Lord and your heart for a career. Ask and you will receive, seek and you will find, and knock and the door will be opened to you (Matt 7:7-11). Third, while you are looking for a job and do not have a job, find what your hand can do and ask God to give you something to do. See what service or ministry you can do and make yourself useful. Help your family with chores. Help a widow or the elderly or someone who needs help. Clean a vacant lot or roadside. Do volunteer work for a church or a charitable or community organization. Assess your gifts and abilities and put these to good use for helping others. Be rich in good works and you will find favor from God and man (Matt 5:16, Titus 3:8,14). Fourth, give to the work of the Lord and the poor. Those who help the poor will be helped by God (Psalm 41:1, Prov 19:17, 28:27, Luke 6:38, Matt 19:21) and those who give to the Church (your spiritual storehouse) will be blessed (Mal 3:10; 2Cor 9:6-11). God wants you to have a good income if He knows you will give to His Church and those in need.

It is very important to have a career and not just a job. A career gives you a better chance of getting a good paying job and a more secure job and being more fulfilled. If you need a career or want a new career, ask God for a career. I cried out to God one season to give me a new career. I spent about six months praying fervently for this, and in my heart I yearned to go into counseling, but I did not see myself being qualified for this, and if I did go into counseling, I wanted it to be a Christian counseling program that was state certified and would help me get a good job.

I waited about six months after this season of prayer, and then I met someone who had gotten a counseling degree from a Christian school that had a state certified counseling program. She told me about the program, and afterwards I kept thinking to myself that I could do this and felt in my heart that this is what I should do. I decided to go through the demanding application process, was accepted, was blessed with a good part time job, earned my master's degree, and got a good paying job afterwards.

The process for finding a career and a good job may not be easy and may take a lot more time than you wanted, but you can do it if you have a clear goal and plans, persevere, believe in yourself, and have faith in God.

In our society it is becoming increasingly more difficult to find fulfilling work. In the old days the vast majority of people worked the land (agriculture or ranching), with the freedom to hunt and fish, and then others were craftsman who made things by hand. If one is able to make a decent living by working the land or by being a craftsman and you do not have to work like a slave, there is much fulfillment in this work. During the industrial revolution many people left the farms and small towns to go to the cities and work in the factories, hoping to make more money and have a more exciting future. However, most of these people found that this factory and clerical work made them feel like robots and did not give them fulfillment.

The reason I am bringing this out is because of my belief that most people do not find a lot of fulfillment in their jobs. Men, especially, look for fulfillment in their work because the male is task oriented (while the female is relationship oriented). If a man cannot find fulfillment in his work, he becomes very discouraged, which can turn into anger or depression, and even not wanting to work at all if one is immature or has bad character. People who do not find fulfillment in their work may not know what to do or even what they are battling, but they need to find fulfillment in some kind of work (vocational, ministry, service) in order to have emotional wholeness. We find purpose in having fulfilling work. If you are not being fulfilled in your vocation, you must find fulfillment somewhere else. Even career counseling books say that most people will have to look outside of their vocational work in order to find fulfillment. This fulfillment can be found in one's family and in doing ministry and volunteer service.

However, it must be understood that even if you are not able to find a job or vocation that is fulfilling, there is a certain measure of fulfillment if your work meets your needs, that it pays the bills and supports you and your family. There is even more fulfillment if this job enables you to have financial wholeness and you are able to give to the church and others. Furthermore, it must be said that there can be great fulfillment in becoming financially independent and even wealthy. This is a blessing from God (Deut 18:8). While money cannot buy happiness, and you can find many rich people who are empty and unfulfilled, money gives you the opportunity to achieve certain things that you could not do without money. It takes money to help people and build the kingdom of God. There is great fulfillment and eternal reward in this, and money gives you the opportunity to achieve this in a more dynamic way.

There is also a certain measure of fulfillment when you do your job with excellence. There is dignity in all work, and if you do your work with excellence, this will develop good character (and excellence is one of the eight spiritual virtues listed in 2Peter 1:5-7). The older I become, the more faith I have that doing any work with excellence, even the lowliest work, is pleasing to God and rewarded by God, and it also earns you respect and favor from man. The Bible says, "Whatever your hand finds to do, do it with all your might" (Eccl 9:10a, NIV; cf. 1Thes 1:3).

You can learn to be excellent in whatever work you do if you do your work as unto the Lord. Paul said,

"[17]And whatever you do in word or deed, do all in the name of the Lord Jesus, giving thanks to God the Father through Him....[23]And whatever you do, do it heartedly, as to the Lord and not to men, [24]knowing that from the Lord you will receive the reward of the inheritance; for you serve the Lord Jesus" (Col 3:17,23-24, NKJV).

Do everything as serving God and be responsible to display the character of God in all that you do. If you do this, you will perform your work and activities with excellence and bring glory to God wherever you might be.

### The Call to Volunteer Service

You can find a certain measure of fulfillment in any work by working as unto the Lord, doing your work with excellence, having your needs met, and being able to give to the church and others, but what if your job does not fulfill you, especially if it is not utilizing your gifts, abilities, and motivations? If you do not have a job that fulfills you, it is imperative that you either look for another job or seek volunteer service or ministry that will fulfill you, although, of course, you should always be engaged in ministry (and your family is your greatest ministry).

Even if you have a fulfilling vocation, besides your ministry, it is good to find volunteer service that helps people. Volunteer service is defined as performing free service in the secular realm (and this service can be your ministry). Volunteer service can include providing oversight to an organization or researching the health and effectiveness of an organization. God calls us to help people and to serve Him through ministry and volunteer service, whether it is through the church or a secular organization.

This is also true for those who are retired and able to live on a retirement plan. You can try to spend your time pursuing happiness in doing what you think is fun, but this will not really fulfill you if this is all you do. You can even refuse to do volunteer service because you hated your job and do not want to ever work again. I know men who worked a job for many years or most of their lives and ended up hating it and could not wait to retire. If you have to take a year off to unwind from your job, this is fine and might be the best thing, but when you come back, you need to volunteer your time to help people and serve God. You can always devote a couple of hours each week to be useful and to help people.

This is also true for those who are disabled. Even if you are disabled, there are still things you can do to be useful and to help people, even if it is just praying. In every church where I have been a member, there was always at least one disabled man or woman who would give his or her time and serve the church faithfully in some way. Identify your gifts, abilities, and motivations and find use for them and make yourself useful. God will even bring opportunities to you for service, and He will do this whether you are disabled, retired, employed, or unemployed.

I was a member of this church that was located about one block away from a group home for abused teenage girls. These girls had to be taken out of their homes because they had been abused and had no one to take care of them. A girl from this home went to the church. I got to talking with her about life at this group home, and she began telling me how the girls were having trouble with math and science. Afterwards I thought about this because I majored in chemistry and minored in math. I felt in my heart that maybe I should try to volunteer there, and so the next week I went with this girl to the home and talked to the house manager about volunteering there as a tutor. I went through the arduous process of applying as a volunteer and was accepted and began tutoring math and science and any other subject those girls needed help in. I can honestly say that this work was the most fulfilling work I have ever had, and I even won an award one year for being selected as one of the top volunteers for that particular organization in the state of Florida. It is the will of God and will even edify you to help those who are weak and in need, wherever that may be.

## Section 4C: Finding Achievement

How do we find fulfilling work (vocation, ministry, service) that will give us purpose and allow us to achieve good things and even great things? There are two basic factors that will help you find the fulfilling work that will bring you achievement and give you purpose in your daily life.[8] First, discover your passion, what you are passionate about and motivated to do. Your passion will usually lead you to fulfilling work, either directly or indirectly (by getting you to the right place). However, passion in itself is not sufficient for finding fulfilling work. This is because you can have many passions and a passion may not be connected to a gift and passions can change if they were based upon emotions. However, finding your passion is absolutely necessary, and you can have more than one passion with these passions working together.

How do you find your passion? It will be in your heart, although when you are immature it is easy to have passions that are according to your emotions and perceptions and not who you are. Thus, it may require practical experiences and soul searching to see your real passions and even your greatest passion. Your passion, however, will always be found in your heart (according to that still and quiet voice in the depths of you, not your loud emotions), and God will speak to your heart about this passion.

---

8- The basic outline for this teaching is from a lecture by John Maxwell that he gave 9/13/2007 at Regent University (Virginia Beach, VA). This lecture was published by the Regent University Keynote newsletter (Vol.3, No.1, 2008). In the newsletter several of his books were cited- *Today Matters, 21 Irrefutable Laws of Leadership, Winning with People, The 360 Degree Leader*.

There can also be two realms of passion in your heart: a passion for God and a passion for vocational work. These two passions can come together for people who have a vocational ministry, but for most people they will be different. Thus, you will have a passion for a certain type of vocation and a passion for a certain type of ministry.

Second, discover your strengths. Your strengths are what you are good at. These are your talents, which are your gifts and abilities. A gift is a natural talent that you are good at. An ability is something that you have learned to do and have become proficient at. For some people, especially when you are young, it may be difficult to see a gift because it can take time to see a gift and gifts have to be developed. The key is to work with the strengths that you see, and in time, even if a strength is not your key gift, it will help you find your key gift and other gifts and abilities, and you can have many gifts and abilities.

How do you discover your strengths? What you like to do will have value for finding a strength, but what you like to do will not always show you a gift. You can get ideas from your education, work and activities. You can also gain insight about yourself by taking a personality, career, or interest assessment.[9] Another way to gain insight about yourself is by receiving counsel from people who know and love you. Finally, you can receive revelation about a strength you have or how to discover a strength by seeking God.

It is important to find your gifts for ministry. We have spiritual gifts. A spiritual gift is a supernatural ability given by God through the Holy Spirit and by His grace and will for the purpose of doing His work. Spiritual gifts are received and activated when you surrender yourself to God and have a heart to do the will of God. Your spiritual gifts will show you what your ministry should be.

There are three major groups of spiritual gifts (Rom 12:6-8, 1Cor 12:8-10, Eph 4:11), and these gifts are contained in the three major passages on the body of Christ (Rom 12:1-8, 1Cor 12:1-31, Eph 4:1-16; see Eph 1:22-23, 4:25, Col 1:18,24, 2:19). Just as the

---

9- These assessments include Strong, Campbell, Kuder, SDS, Myers-Briggs, Florida Choices Planner Interest Profiler and Career Planner. These assessments are usually based upon the personality types developed by Jung and Holland. You can also be helped by studying the four temperaments (choleric, sanguine, phlegmatic, melancholy). See *Spirit Controlled Temperament* by Tim LaHaye.

human body is one body with many parts that have different functions, so too the body of Christ is one body with many members who have different gifts and ministries. This means that the Church is an organism and not an organization. Every follower of Jesus Christ has at least one spiritual gift and is called to serve and to be a minister. Therefore, as Paul exhorted Timothy, "do not neglect the gift that is in you" (1Tim 4:14, NKJV), but "fan into flame the gift of God, which is in you" and do not be afraid to help others, "for God did not give us a spirit of timidity, but a spirit of power, of love, and of self discipline" (2Tim 1:6-7, NIV). It is important, therefore, to find your spiritual gifts and ministry.

How can you find your spiritual gifts and ministry? First, be surrendered to God and be willing to obey Him ("Lord, I will serve You, use me"). Second, seek the Lord through prayer, worship, and the Word about what God made you to do in life (your destiny) and how you can serve Him (your assignments). Third, see past successes and what has fulfilled you as a guide. Fourth, see the pain and tribulation that you have gone through, for it is in the pain and tribulation that you have been through that God will use you to help others (2Cor 1:3-10). Five, be led by your heart (following the quiet voice deep within you that is God speaking to you) and learn to step out in faith. If you follow these principles, you will discover your spiritual gifts and ministry.

The key for finding fulfilling work (vocation, ministry, and service) is finding your strengths and passions. When you find your strengths and passions, this will help you find work that will fulfill you and lead to achievement and give you purpose in what you do (the "how" of life). Find the things that you are good at and even best at and connect them with your passions. When you do this, you will find the work that you should be doing in life for vocation, ministry, and service.

When you are doing the work and ministry that you are supposed to be doing in life, this gives you much purpose and energizes you and you will see yourself fulfilling your destiny. When you believe you are not fulfilling your destiny in life, you feel stuck and in a pit or you feel you are going around in circles and not getting anywhere. This is when discouragement sets in, and, in time, hopelessness and despair can grip your heart.

Are you fulfilling your destiny in life and in God? You fulfill your destiny when you obey God and do the will of God, and you obey God and do the will of God by losing your life for Christ. Are you fulfilling the will of God for your life? You must know this because we are rewarded for our works (Matt 6:19-24, 25:31-46, Rom 14:7-12, 1Cor 3:10-15, Heb 6:10, 1Pet 1:17), although it is important to understand that what you do for God, which includes how you live for God, will depend upon how much you have been transformed into the image of Christ. Thus, what you do will be determined by what you be. Therefore, focus on your inner person and not works, but realize that you will be judged and rewarded by what you do according to what you have been given. Thus, find out what God wants you to do and do it, and when you fulfill the will of God for your life, you will fulfill your destiny in God.

When you have discovered the work (vocation, ministry, and service) that gives you purpose, there are two factors that will help you become successful in this work. First, grow to your maximum potential in this work. You do this by practicing and developing the skills for this work. When you identify your strengths, be the best you can be in these areas, and it is even good to become a specialist. It is also useful to have goals and a plan for what you need to improve upon and how you will make these improvements.

What you are willing to spend your time on and work hard at to develop your skills will confirm your passion. If you are not willing to work hard at something in order to become better at it, then either this is not what you are meant to do in life or you have a serious problem with laziness. Your attitude must be: I will be the best I can be in this work. This means that you must invest in yourself. Work to improve your knowledge, abilities, gifts, skills, character, and mental wholeness. You must always be working to become a better person, and this improvement should be in all areas (mental, emotional, physical, relational, and spiritual).

Second, the other factor that will help you become successful is to seek to help or benefit others (and this includes God). We must live to love God (worshiping, following His ways, building His kingdom) and to love people. If you have a vocation that does not benefit people very much, you might wonder how you can benefit others through this vocation. If you earn good money, you can benefit people by giving a greater share of your money to God and those who need help. If you have a vocation that does not benefit people very much and do not make enough money, you can focus more on ministry or volunteer service to help others. Finally, you can help others through just the people you meet each day. Like the good Samaritan (Luke 10:25-37), did you stop for that one and minister what God wanted you to say or do for that person?

God commands us to love others, and we preach this in the Church, but what is love? Successful people focus their time and effort on what they can give to others and how they can add value to others, believing that success is determined by the seeds that they sow in others. This might be the opposite of what you see, for people (especially leaders) tend to use others for what can be extracted from them, but this is not loving people. Focus on how you can help and give to others and how you can help others be successful. Your eternal rewards really are determined by the seeds that you sow into others, not the harvest or help that you try to extract from them. Finally, it must be understood that the most important sphere for helping people is to take care of your family. Are you investing time in your family and working to help them be successful? While it is important to get outside of your four walls and help others, it is a true word that charity begins at home.

There are four things that successful people do in relation to helping and benefiting others. First, successful people form relationships with the people they work with and are associated with. Second, successful people equip others by helping to improve their skills and character and giving them the opportunity to grow. Third, successful people have a positive attitude and a humble spirit and see the good in others and their gifts. Fourth, successful people exhibit leadership by positively influencing people, focusing on encouraging and building people up. The essence of leadership is the ability to influence people. You can be a leader if you love people and work to help and benefit those around you. Your greatest achievement in life is helping and benefiting others and being a positive influence to people, not what positions you held or how much money you made.

When people are at the end of their lives, especially if they are on their death beds, other than the issue of one's eternal destiny, people are concerned about the issue of love. They are concerned about whether they loved others and were loved by others. The overriding question is: Did I love others well and did others love me well? If you helped and benefited others and treated them with respect and looked out for their interests, then you can be sure that you have loved others and others have loved and appreciated you.

You can ask yourself this same question concerning your relationship with God (knowing that God loves you with an everlasting love): Did I love God well and was I at rest in His love? You can rephrase this question by asking: Did I love God by worshiping and obeying Him (doing His will) and did I trust Him?

We should seek to help and benefit God. This is loving God. When we love God, we will focus on serving God, building the kingdom of God, and bringing glory to God. You serve God by living for God and doing the will of God. You build the kingdom of God by bringing people into the kingdom and building up those who are in the kingdom and promoting kingdom principles in society. You bring glory to God by worshiping and trusting God. If you follow these principles, you will achieve great things for God.

Loving God and loving others helps us see what is important in life and what has eternal significance. It is important to believe that we are doing that which is important and achieving things that have eternal significance. Importance can be defined as what will help or benefit God and others. Eternal significance can be defined as establishing a foundation for future work or passing on something of value to the next generation or doing what will last forever. We must believe that we are doing something important and achieving something that will have lasting consequences (at least for some of the people we deal with). If you do not believe that you are engaged in some type of work that is important and is achieving eternal purposes, it will be difficult to find fulfillment and purpose in life. The most important work and what will achieve eternal significance is loving God and loving people, and when we do this, we will know and be doing the will of God and we will be working to build the kingdom of God.

You must live for a cause that is greater than you and you must live for and worship someone who is greater than you. You can live for yourself and find a season of happiness in this, for there is great deception when you get and do what you want and self is the boss, but in the end you will not find lasting purpose and fulfillment. You must live for what has eternal significance and for the God who created you. This will bring you the greatest fulfillment and achievement in life.

In this world there are many different kinds of kingdoms that people try to build. People will try to build their own kingdom or worship a kingdom that looks majestic and wonderful. Some people are centered around the Magic Kingdom, paying homage to the mouse. Some try to build a political kingdom, but if their governing is not built upon biblical principles, it will fail in the end. Others have a humanitarian or philanthropic goal and will try to build a great society kingdom that will help people and make this world a better place to live. This is a worthy endeavor, but if it is not based upon biblical principles and is not in the hands of the righteous, in the end it will not achieve its intended purposes. It is noble and mandated by God to do good deeds, but we must remember to do work that is established upon biblical principles and has eternal purposes and the future in mind, for this is the work that will have eternal significance and achieve the greatest things.

What kingdom are you building and who are you serving? The most important kingdom is the kingdom of God and the most important service is serving and worshiping God. Are you loving God and loving people and working to build the kingdom of God? This is what will bring you the greatest achievement in life.[10]

When you find fulfilling work and ministry, you will find fulfillment and purpose and begin to find achievement, and when you strive to be the best you can be and seek to help or benefit others, you will find excellence, success, and great achievement. Finally, when you love God and others and do the will of God and work to build the kingdom of God, you will find achievement that will last forever and receive eternal rewards.

---

10- How do you accomplish a work or complete a project? The following is a good format (using the story of the rebuilding of the walls of Jerusalem by Nehemiah). These principles are: 1) see a need (1:1-2), 2) spiritual preparation through prayer and the Word (1:3-11), 3) secure authority (2:1-10), 4) examine the situation and determine the resources needed (2:11-16), 5) formulate a plan, 6) give your vision to others and exhort them to be a part of the work (2:17-20), 7) secure the resources (people and materials), 8) organize the people and the work (3:1-32), 9) put the project into action, 10) overcome obstacles (4:1-6:14), 11) finish the project or the project phase (6:15-16), 12) evaluate the results.

## Summary: The Search for Achievement

A. Defining achievement and work: Achievement is accomplishing something significant or worthy. We find achievement through work. Work is engaging in any activity or task that is doing something useful. It is good to work and we are exhorted to be rich in good deeds by using our talents. We find purpose in having fulfilling work.

B. The domains of work:
1. The call to ministry: We are sons of God clothed with Christ and have been given spiritual gifts to minister to others.
2. The call to vocation and work: Vocational work gives you self esteem and the ability to support yourself and a family and to give to those in need and the work of God. Money is important. It takes money to live and to build the kingdom of God. Be salt and light in the workplace. Be diligent in finding a good job and career that meets your needs and uses your talents, but you may need to find fulfillment outside of your job.
3. The call to volunteer service: This service can be your ministry. It gives you the opportunity to reach out to the helpless and needy in your community that you cannot do through a church.

C. Finding Achievement:
1. Find your passions and strengths.
2. Become the best you can be in this work.
3. Focus on helping or benefiting people. Your harvest will come from helping others be successful. This focus should also be with God. Are you working to help and benefit God?
4. Invest your time in what has eternal significance. What kingdom are you building? Are you working to build the kingdom of God?
5. Working and doing good is how you obey God and do the will of God, and when you obey God and do the will of God, you will fulfill your calling and destiny in life.

# Appendix: The Spiritual Gifts

There are three major lists of spiritual gifts: the ascension gifts of Christ (Eph 4:7,8,11), the functional or ministry gifts of God (Rom 12:3-8), and the manifestations or gifts of the Holy Spirit (1Cor 12:7-11). The ascension gifts of Christ are: apostle, prophet, evangelist, pastor, and teacher. These are gifts of spiritual leadership and authority for perfecting and equipping the saints. The functional or ministry gifts of God are: prophecy, serving, teaching, encouraging, giving, managing, and mercy. These gifts are the seven fundamental ways in which we function or minister in the body of Christ in ministering the word of God and doing service. The gifts of the Holy Spirit are: word of wisdom, word of knowledge, faith, workings of miracles, gifts of healings, prophecy, discerning of spirits, tongues, and interpretation of tongues. These gifts are the manifestations of the presence and power of the Holy Spirit.

The ascension gifts are called "the ascension gifts of Christ" because they are "gifts (*domata*)" given by "Christ" to men and women "when He ascended" into heaven (Eph 4:7-8). While these gifts are given by God's grace, they are not *charismata* gifts that are available to every believer. Thus, not every believer will receive an ascension gift. These gifts are also called "the office gifts" (for they are leadership offices) and "the five-fold ministry" (for there are five of them). These gifts have also been called "the ministry gifts" (for they are services), but this term has been out of style and is now used for the functional gifts of God.

The ascension gifts of Christ are gifts of spiritual leadership and authority that are given by Christ to lead the Church and to perfect and equip the saints. These are gifts given by the grace and will of God, not offices or positions of governmental authority that have been ordained by man. These gifts must be imparted, activated, and directed by the Holy Spirit. The ascension gifts are

115

separate from the offices of church government (overseer, elder, deacon), which are positions for governing a church or denomination. One can receive an ascension gift without being ordained an elder in a church, and one can have an office of church government without having an ascension gift.

The ministry gifts of Romans 12 are called "the functional gifts of God" because Paul uses *praxis* (SC-#4234), which means "function, practice" (Rom 12:4), and they are "gifts (*charismata*)" that "God has allotted" to us (Rom 12:3,6). These gifts have also been called "the motivational gifts" because, if one has the gift, one will become motivated for this ministry. However, the term "motivational" is not an accurate term because it is common to be motivated for a ministry without having the gift. They are also called "the grace gifts" because we are given "different gifts according to the grace given to us" (Rom 12:6) and we are given "a measure of faith" for the gift we are given (Rom 12:3).

The term "functional" might sound too technical and is rarely used, but it is the term that Paul uses to describe these gifts. The term "motivational" is not the best term for them, for you can be motivated for one of these ministries and not have the gift. The term "ministry" could be used to refer to these gifts because it describes these gifts very well and does not sound technical and is a term that is no longer used for the ascension gifts. Therefore, these gifts can also be called "the ministry gifts of God."

The functional or ministry gifts of God are the seven fundamental ways in which we function or minister in the body of Christ in ministering the word of God and doing service. When you become born of the Spirit, one of these seven gifts is imparted into you. While these gifts may be consistent with the abilities and qualities that one is born with, they are still supernatural gifts and not natural abilities or inclinations. We are not born with these gifts. They must be imparted, activated, and directed by the Holy Spirit. Everyone who is born of the Spirit has at least one functional gift. This gift determines how you function in the body of Christ and will be the foundation of your ministry perspective and leadership style (for everyone can lead in what one is gifted in). You should try to identify your primary functional gift. This will greatly benefit you in finding your ministry and fulfilling your calling in God.

Since these gifts are the seven fundamental ministries of the Church, every believer can have a role in each ministry. Thus, everyone can become motivated for all seven ministries. As we fulfill a role in one of these ministries, God can equip us to do an adequate job, and it may even be possible to manifest the gift on occasion (which is not having the gift but the gift being in operation), but there are those who have the gift who will be specially anointed in this ministry.

A functional gift is a gift that one can function in on a regular and continual basis according to one's faith (Rom 12:3). One can always manifest a functional gift and press into that ministry without having to have a special anointing of the Holy Spirit, for the gift is in you (although prophecy works somewhat differently since it requires faith and is also a gift of the Spirit, and this will be explained later). One can always manifest the gift if one is submitted to the Holy Spirit and has faith. Thus, this gift can be practiced according to the will of the one who is gifted.

There is a special relationship between the ascension gifts of Christ and the functional or ministry gifts of God. Each ascension gift has a corresponding functional gift. This functional gift serves as the core gift or function of the ascension gift, and by itself (for those who do not have an ascension gift) will function as a junior ministry in relation to the corresponding ascension gift. The functional gift is similar in ministry to its corresponding ascension gift, but the sphere of ministry and the spiritual leadership and authority in leading the Church and perfecting and equipping the saints is much greater for the ascension gift.

The ascension/functional gift pairs are: Teacher-teaching, Pastor-encouraging, Evangelist-mercy, Prophet-prophecy, Apostle-managing. The other two functional gifts, serving and giving, do not correspond to any ascension gift but are paired with each other. These two gifts, along with the office of deacon, comprise the "helps" ministry of the Church (1Cor 12:28). The "helps" ministry provides the necessary labor and resources that a church needs in order to function properly.

The manifestations or gifts of 1Corinthians 12 are called "the gifts of the Holy Spirit" or "the gifts of the Spirit" (the abbreviated form) because they are "gifts (*charismata*)" (1Cor 12:4,31) that are given to us through "the Spirit" (1Cor 12:4,7,8,9,13), that is, "the

Spirit of God" or "the Holy Spirit" (12:3). They are also called "the manifestation gifts of the Spirit" or "the manifestations of the Holy Spirit" because Paul calls each one a "manifestation of the Spirit" (1Cor 12:7). Paul said that "the manifestation of the Spirit is given to each one for the profit of all" (1Cor 12:7). Thus, there is the sense that these are manifestations that flow out of the Spirit filled believer. Because these are manifestations of the Spirit, every believer can manifest each one for one's own benefit, but when the manifestation is for the benefit of another, it is called a gift. They are also called "the sign gifts" because they are signs of the tangible presence and activity of the Holy Spirit.

Because these are *charismata* ("grace gifts"), every believer can receive them. However, they are given according to the will of God, for the apostle Paul said, "But one and the same Spirit works all these things, distributing to each one individually as He wills" (1Cor 12:11, NKJV; cf. 12:18, Luke 5:17, Heb 2:4). He then makes an analogy between these gifts and the human body, saying that just as the body has many parts with different operations, the body of Christ has many members with different gifts (1Cor 12:12-31). Thus, these are manifestations of the Holy Spirit that proceed by the will of God. This means that these gifts cannot be forced or guaranteed. We receive these gifts when we have faith for them and are surrendered to God to be used in them and "earnestly desire" them to bring glory to God and to help others (1Cor 12:31, 14:1,12). These gifts can be manifested any time after we become born of the Spirit. God wants these gifts to be manifested among His people, and these gifts will flow from Spirit filled believers as long as the will of God is being accomplished by their manifestation.

Prophecy is both a gift of the Holy Spirit and a functional gift of God and will work as a combination of these two types of gifts. If one is able to function in the gift of prophecy, one is able to press into prophecy through prayer and worship and being submitted to the Spirit, but one still cannot force or guarantee prophecy. This means that you prophesy according to your faith and that prophecy must end when one's faith ends (Rom 12:6), and the ending of one's faith can be caused by the Holy Spirit terminating the gift. Thus, if you can function in the gift of prophecy, you can press into prophecy until the Holy Spirit decides to terminate the gift or you become too tired to stay in the anointing of the Spirit.

What is the relationship between these three groups of gifts? The relationship between these gifts could be described by using the analogy of a Christmas tree. The ascension gifts of Christ, being the leadership, would be the trunk. The functional or ministry gifts of God, being the services, would be the branches. The gifts of the Holy Spirit, being the signs of the presence and power of the Holy Spirit, would be the lights and ornaments. It should be noted that the Trinity is seen in these three groups of gifts- "the functional gifts of God [the Father]", "the ascension gifts of Christ [the Son]", and "the manifestation gifts of the Holy Spirit".*

---

* For indepth teaching on the spiritual gifts, see: *The Spiritual Gifts (Part 1): The Ascension Gifts of Christ and the Functional Gifts of God* and *The Spiritual Gifts (Part 2): The Gifts of the Holy Spirit* by Tim Williams.

# Preview

The following pages are two page previews of chapters 5 to 12.

Chapter 5

# The Search for Love

You were created for love. Every cell of your being cries out for love, to love and to be loved, and if you are not receiving love or you have a love deficit in your heart, you will battle emptiness and loneliness every day of your life.[1]

We have a need for love, and love is one of the three ways that we find purpose in life. We have a need to belong to a family and to have a home, a place where we can find acceptance, comfort, security, affirmation, and identity and be established in our destiny. We have a need for meaningful relationships. This need for meaningful relationships and to belong to a family includes both people and God. We must love and be loved by others, and we must love and feel loved by God. It is appropriate that the two greatest commandments are to love God and to love others as yourself (Matt 22:37-40, Mark 12:29-31).

Love is the most important thing in life. It is the most important thing about who we are and what we need (whether you see this or not). Love is our greatest need. This is why the greatest pain in the world is not having love and not knowing where to find love. If you cannot find love and you do not feel loved, you will feel disconnected from others and the world, you will struggle to find purpose, hope, and meaning in life, and you will battle emptiness and loneliness every day of your life.

Love gives us the greatest meaning in life. This is why if you cannot find love, you will not find meaning. You will also not find purpose, for you will have no one to belong to and give to. The

---

1- While the outline of this chapter is my own work with much fresh material, I am indebted to the teachings of Jack Frost, primarily his teaching, *Experiencing the Father's Embrace*, which has had a profound affect upon my life. The ministry founded by Jack and Trisha Frost is Shiloh Place Ministries (PO Box 5; Conway, SC 29528; 843-365-8990; shilohplace.org).

pain of not having love and not feeling loved can even be greater than the pain of having a miserable life with nothing to do or gain. This is because, if you have love, you will always have something good in your life and you will always have hope for the future. The apostle Paul was right when he said that love is the greatest and love is eternal (1Cor 13:13).

You were created in love as well as for love. It was in the heart of God to create children who could have a love relationship with Him. This is why there is a searching within us to know our Creator God and why we must have faith in God in order to find meaning in life. When God created man and woman, God created us in His image (Gen 1:26-27). If we are created in the image of God, then it is important to ask who God is. The Bible says that "God is love" (1John 4:8,16). If God is love and He created us in His image, then God created us in love and for love.

Love is our greatest need, and if this need is not being met, it will cause great pain, and this pain will rule your life and drive you. When the need for love is not being met and a love deficit develops in your heart, you will have many problems. When you have a love deficit in your heart and your desire for love is not balanced with truth and wisdom, you are easily deceived and you will make bad choices and wrong decisions. You will be driven to run after temporal affections in order to find love or fill the emptiness, for pain seeks pleasure and pain seeks comfort.

When you have a love deficit in your heart, you will battle oppression every day of your life with constant issues of inner pain and loneliness. This oppression will manifest itself by constant battles with anger, bitterness, depression, hopelessness, shame, guilt, fear, or anxiety. When you have a love deficit in your heart, you will experience much insecurity, either being uncomfortable with emotional intimacy or becoming overly attached to others in a dysfunctional way. Your relationships will then be based on duty or the fear of loneliness rather than on love. You may constantly compete for attention and have a need for approval with a fear of rejection, and you may see any counsel as condemnation. You may constantly struggle with the fear of others, the fear of failure, and the fear of not being perfect. A love deficit in your heart, especially if you experience feelings of loneliness or not feeling loveable, can drive you into unhealthy emotions and dysfunctional behavior.

Chapter 6

# The Search for Maturity

We have a need for maturity, and so there is a search for maturity. We have a need to feel that we are mature, and we want to believe that we are making improvements in life and becoming a better person. What is maturity? Maturity is being fully developed or being at the end stage of development. Maturity is advancing to a desired stage or reaching a high position or quality. Maturity is being completed or perfected. Maturity is having full power or stature. Maturity is attaining a final state. Maturity is reaching your full potential.

Maturity, however, is not just a state; it is also a process. This means that maturity can be relative, being judged by others or your peer group as having attained a certain level or ability. For the mental, emotional, and spiritual growth of human beings, maturity is more of a process than a final state, and although you can come to the place where others see you as mature, maturity is a never ending process. Thus, maturity is a road that you walk. If you are walking on the road to maturity, it can be said that you are mature.

There is something inside of us that yearns to reach our full potential. We hate the thought of remaining an inferior or lesser person or not having full freedom or stature or not attaining what we believe we are capable of doing. Thus, we strive to improve ourselves and to become more competent. This process of self improvement is one of the three main ways that we find purpose in life. You will find purpose if you keep trying to improve yourself.

If you have quit trying to improve yourself, it is usually because you have allowed disappointment or the cares and worries of life to overcome you. You must always be improving yourself and strive every day and every year to become a better person. It is the mature thinking person who knows that one must always be working to improve oneself and to become a better person.

123

Therefore, the way to maturity is self improvement. Self improvement is improving yourself and your life, and this should be in all areas of life (mental, emotional, relational, physical, financial, spiritual). Self improvement is becoming a better person in character, personality, and ability. This is becoming a more mature person. Self improvement is also building a better life for yourself and your loved ones. You must improve yourself in order to mature. There is a natural desire to improve yourself, and you will find that self improvement will give you much purpose and fulfillment in life. The best investment that you can make is to improve yourself and become a better person.

When we make a decision to follow Jesus Christ, to be His disciple, self improvement is growing spiritually and becoming more like Christ. This is discipleship. This is the most important self improvement that you can make in your life, although, of course, it is a work of God in your heart as much as it is a personal discipline (and more will be said later about self discipline). The primary focus of this chapter will be searching for spiritual maturity.

While spiritual maturity (becoming more like Christ) is the most important aspect of maturity, it is important that we grow and improve ourselves in every aspect of life. You really cannot separate the spiritual from the practical, for you will find that self improvement in the practical aspects of life, especially personal growth, will help you improve your spiritual life and gifts. This proved true for me when I worked at the boys prison.

During the two and half years that I worked at the prison, I did not do any preaching in church. I was not happy about this and thought that my preaching skills would suffer. After I left I sought the Lord for a message to preach, and about two months later I was able to preach. I was very nervous and had trouble following my outline, and when I finished, I was not satisfied with the presentation. My pastor, however, exclaimed how I had such confidence in my speaking, a confidence I never had before, and I even saw this myself.

This word triggered my memory of a revelation I had when I left the prison. I sensed in my heart that I had a lot more confidence in myself than when I started there. Working at the prison had given me more self confidence. This confidence came

Chapter 7

# The Search for Humility

We have a need for humility, but humility is one quality that we do not initially seek after. This is because we start out in life being self centered. Initially, this is not a problem, for each individual starts out in life truly thinking that the world revolves around oneself. This is the thinking of a child. There comes a time, however, when you realize that life does not center around you. You realize that if you want to have a happier life, you must get rid of pride and get some humility in you. It is only then that you search for humility and try not to be self centered.

Humility is the goal of this chapter, but the search for humility can be a fruitless search because humility is one of those virtues that is difficult to attain by seeking after it. If you try to be humble, you might not become humble, and you might even become more proud. The Bible exhorts us to strive for humility and to humble ourselves before God, but it takes a work of God in your heart to produce a humble spirit. While we must practice humility, the road to humility is being convicted of the pride in your heart and then resolving to get rid of this pride by losing self centeredness. There is a real search for humility and we must practice humility, but we will find humility by focusing on getting rid of pride through losing self centeredness.

In the introductory chapter it was noted that there are at least seven basic factors that contribute to mental wholeness, with losing self centeredness being one of them. What is self centeredness? Self centeredness means that you see yourself at the center. Self centeredness is exhibited in pride, conceit, arrogance, selfishness, control, intimidation, manipulation, self exaltation, judgment, condemnation. Self centeredness does not respect others, does not respect the boundaries of others, and blames others for problems. Self centeredness is having to have things your way (or people can hit the highway). Self centeredness is putting yourself first and being domineering (3John 1:9-10). Self centeredness is thinking only about your own interests and rights with little or no concern for others. Self centeredness is being a lover of money and pleasure and what self wants (2Tim 3:1-5). Self centeredness has a low view of others, especially for those who are different or are perceived as being weaker. Self centeredness is seeing yourself as superior to others and that you are the standard and the center for how people should be. These are all aspects of self centeredness. You must lose self centeredness in order to develop humility.

What is humility? Humility is modesty, being down to earth, self-effacing (unassuming), unselfishness, selflessness, mutuality (submitting to one another), gentleness, helpfulness, meekness (power under control). Humility is being conscious of one's defects and shortcomings (seeing your weaknesses). Humility is not seeing yourself as better than others. Humility is not thinking too highly of yourself and seeing others as having the same worth that you have. Humility is making yourself low. Humility is being gentle in how you act toward others and giving up things for the good of others. Humility is caring about the interests of others and not using others. Humility is denying self and being a servant to help others. Humility is being free from the bondage of always having to get your way and what you want. These are all aspects of humility. Humility is an important trait for getting along with people and living a good life and opens the way for love, gentleness, kindness, mercy, and respecting others.

The key description of humility is not being proud. Humility is the opposite of pride. Pride is the root of self centeredness. Pride is the deadliest sin and the original sin (Prov 11:2, 16:18*, 22:4, 29:23, Isa 14:3-17, Ezek 28:1-19). Pride goes before a fall. You can be walking with God, but if you become puffed up in your view of yourself and your importance, you will become arrogant and fall into sin. Pride is considered to be the root of selfishness and being in love with this world (James 4:1-10, 1John 2:15-17, 2Tim 3:1-5). It can be seen in life that pride leads to sin, arrogance and an evil heart always go together, and people soon despise a person who is proud. This is a description of the one who is proud.

Humility is important for living in the grace of God, for "God resists the proud but gives grace to the humble" (James 4:6, 1Pet

## Chapter 8

# The Search for Self Worth

We have a need for self worth, to feel that one has worth as a person and that one's life has significance, and so there is a search for self worth. When you cannot find self worth or you find self worth in what is not healthy, you become pulled and pushed by the forces of this world and those around you. It is as though your life is like a boat without a rudder and you become driven and dragged every which way by the currents and winds you come into contact with. If you are smart, you learn to stay to yourself, but you still have to deal with self worth and reaching your full potential.

We live in a society that is focused on self worth and places much emphasis on self worth, but too many times it is a self worth that rests upon a foundation of sand and will ultimately lead to a crisis of self worth. Self worth must be established upon humility or else you will become puffed up with yourself and fall. Self worth must also be established upon a relationship with God or else you will be deceived and end up falling. Thus, self worth is feeling good about yourself while having a right view of yourself.

Self worth can be described in the following ways. Self worth is believing that you have worth and are a worthwhile human being. Self worth is having confidence in yourself and feeling good about yourself. Self worth is considering yourself to have value and that your life matters and has significance. Self worth is respecting yourself. Self worth is accepting who you are and starting your life journey from this point. Self worth is seeing yourself as somebody and as worthy as anyone else. Self worth is believing that you are a capable human being who can be useful. Self worth is believing that you are needed and appreciated. Self worth is believing that you have the potential to be successful. Self worth is cherishing yourself and not allowing others to use you. Self worth is seeing yourself as attractive in your own special way.

Self worth is feeling empowered and not helpless. Self worth is believing that you are loveable and accepted. Self worth is believing that you came from God. These all describe self worth.

How do we find self worth and how is self worth attained? You can find self worth in many ways, and there are both healthy and unhealthy ways to find self worth. We will first look at the unhealthy ways. We human beings have a tendency to base our self worth on these three things- performance, talent, and approval from others. Performance is achieving things and being successful and living up to certain standards. Talent is one's abilities, gifts, and personal appearance. Approval is when others like you and think you are a worthwhile person by being your judge. These can all build your self worth on a foundation of sinking sand.

When you derive your self worth from your performance, you will focus on what you achieve and how successful you are in order to feel good about yourself. If you are not successful and do not achieve your dreams and goals and do not meet certain standards, then you feel that you are a failure and unworthy. When you derive your self worth from your talents, you will focus on your gifts and abilities and outer person in order to feel good about yourself. If you do not measure up to others, then you feel inferior and maybe even worthless. When you derive your self worth from the approval of others, you focus on what others think or say about you in order to feel good about yourself and you strive for how you can please others. You live your life by trying to please others, to make them happy, and then if people do not affirm you or approve of you, you feel rejected and might see yourself as a nobody.

Those who were brought up in a home where there was a lot of anger, negativity, criticism, or judgment, especially if there was abuse, neglect, or abandonment, are especially prone to seek approval. A condemning spirit gets into your heart so that you do not think right about yourself and do not feel good about yourself. This lack of self worth can then be a factor in driving you to dysfunctional behavior or the wrong people, people who may accept anybody (if you do what they want) and tolerate anything but will lead you down the wrong path.

Living life by trying to find self worth through the approval of others or by one's performance or talents will place you under heavy weights and tremendous pressures. These pressures and

Chapter 9

# The Search for Freedom (part 1)

We have a need for freedom. There are different kinds of freedom, but the freedom that will be discussed in this chapter, which is the greatest freedom you can have, is having a free heart. You can be a free person and have the freedom to choose and do what you want to do, but if your heart is not free, you will live as one who is in bondage. On the other hand, you can be in prison, but if your heart is free, you can live as someone who is free. There is also a false freedom. You can feel free or think you are free, but not really be free in your heart. It is having a free heart that is the most important freedom.

You can cry out for freedom, but is your heart free? When Christ came into the world, the Messianic expectations of the Jewish people were very high and they were crying out for freedom from the Roman Empire. They were expecting a Messiah who would come as a conquering King and rescue them from their enemies and the bondage of Rome. However, when Jesus rode into Jerusalem the week before the Passover, he did not ride in on a great white horse with an armed band of soldiers following him. Instead, he rode into the city on a lowly donkey, a young colt that had never been ridden. The mother donkey was walking along with him, but there was no army. This fulfilled a prophecy in Zechariah. Matthew quotes it, saying,

"Tell the daughter of Zion, 'Behold, your King is coming to you, lowly, and sitting on a donkey, a colt, the foal of a donkey'" (Matt 21:5, NKJV, see Zech 9:9; cf. Matt 21:1-11, Mark 11:1-11, Luke 19:28-44, John 12:12-19).[1]

---

1- The Greek word translated as "lowly" is *praus* (SC-#4239, adj.), which means "meek" (Matt 5:5, 11:29, 21:5, 1Pet 3:4, LXX Psalm 37:11). It is the meek who will inherit the earth (Mt 5:5). See fn#2 for definition of "meekness".

Jesus came as a meek and lowly Messiah and not as a conquering King (Isaiah 52:13-53:12), and he came as the Savior of the world (Matt 1:21, Luke 1:76-79, 2:11,28-32, John 4:42, Acts 4:12, 5:31, 13:23), for there was a greater bondage than the bondage of the Roman Empire. This was the bondage to sin and the kingdom of darkness (the ruler being Satan). People's hearts first needed to be set free from the bondage of sin and the kingdom of darkness. This reveals even more that the most important freedom is for your heart to be free.

Your heart is free when you are able to live in love, joy, peace, patience, kindness, goodness, faith, meekness,[2] and self control. These are the fruit of the Spirit (Gal 5:22-23). Now, nobody is perfect in these traits, but we are exhorted to aim for perfection (Matt 5:48, 2Cor 13:11, Col 1:28). It is a walk in the Spirit (Gal 5:24-25). When we live in the Spirit and not the flesh, there is freedom. The apostle Paul said, "Now the Lord is the Spirit, and where the Spirit of the Lord is, there is freedom" (2Cor 3:17, NIV; Gal 5:1). While we can never be perfect, the more you live in the Spirit, the more freedom you will have in your heart, and the more your heart is free, the more you will find fulfillment. You must understand that your heart must be free in order to find fulfillment. Thus, there is a real and intense search for freedom of the heart.

---

2- The Greek word is *prautes* (SC-#4240, noun), which means "meekness" (1Cor 4:21, 2Cor 10:1, Gal 5:23, 6:1 Eph 4:2, Col 3:12 1Tim 6:11, 2Tim 2:25, Titus 3:2, James 1:21, 3:13, 1Pet 3:15). Meekness is power under control, and in relation to God, meekness is submission to God that is exhibited in gentleness and humility toward others. Meekness is a difficult word to define in English, for it signifies weakness in our culture, but it was a positive trait in ancient Greece and is even a fruit of the Spirit (Gal 5:23). This negative meaning in our culture and the fact that this word has strong connotations of humility and gentleness is probably why this word is usually translated as "gentleness" or "humility" in the modern translations. However, it cannot be translated as "humility" because there is a Greek word for "humility" (*tapeinophrosyne*, SC-#5012) and it cannot be translated as "gentleness" because there is a Greek word for "gentleness" (*epieikeias*, SC-#1932). It must be noted that these three words (meekness, humility, gentleness) are all used in one verse (2Cor 10:1), and also meekness and humility are used together (Matt 11:29, Eph 4:2 & Col 3:12) and gentleness and meekness are used together (Titus 3:2). Therefore, this word must be translated as "meekness". It must be noted that this is one of those words whose spelling was changing during the first century A.D. The older forms are *praotes* (SC-#4236) and *praos* (SC-#4235).

# Chapter 10

# The Search for Freedom (part 2)

### Section 10A: Spiritual Weapons

"³For though we walk in the flesh, we do not war according to the flesh. ⁴For the weapons of our warfare are not carnal but mighty in God for pulling down strongholds, ⁵casting down arguments and every high thing that exalts itself against the knowledge of God, bringing every thought into captivity to the obedience of Christ" (2Cor 10:3-5, NKJV).

In order to tear down strongholds of wrong thinking and remove bad roots in the soul and bring healing to the soul, we must use spiritual weapons or tools and we must bring every thought into captivity to the obedience of Christ. Bringing a thought into captivity to the obedience of Christ is putting down the thought (even telling yourself to put the thought down) and bringing your thoughts into line with the knowledge of God through prayer, worship, declarations, and the Word of God. This is what will tear down the strongholds of wrong thinking and pull out the bad roots and bring true and lasting change, deliverance, and healing.

People are always asking God to change them or to deliver them from an addiction or a life controlling problem, but the reality is that there may be no change or deliverance. People will then conclude that they are not good enough or God is not there for them and will quit trying. If there is no change or deliverance, the problem is usually because one is being driven by pain, bitterness, or judgments, and until the pain is resolved and the bitterness and judgments are confessed and put down (renounced), there will be no change or deliverance, at least change or deliverance that is lasting.

It is true that the anointing breaks the yoke, but many times the yoke is caused by our own wrong thinking and the bad roots we are holding in our soul. The yoke of oppression can be broken off by the anointing, but if you do not resolve the pain and the bitterness and the judgments that caused the oppression, the yoke will come back again (but do continue getting the oppression broken off of you).[1]

When the root of the problem is unresolved pain, bitterness, and judgment, change or deliverance usually will not come forth by you crying out for change or deliverance. Instead, it usually comes forth by seeking God and receiving revelation from the Lord about what to do and speaking the Word of God by the Holy Spirit. God has crucified the old nature through faith in Jesus Christ, but you must crucify the old thoughts and ways of thinking and the lies that you have embraced. Taking a thought captive and making it obedient to Christ is putting off the old self and putting on the new self (Eph 4:22-24).

There are three basic spiritual weapons or tools for finding lasting change and deliverance and healing for the soul. There is the Word of God, the Spirit of God, and the People of God. The Word of God means that you read, hear, study, and meditate upon the Word of God and then you obey or follow this Word to the best of your ability. The Spirit of God means that the Holy Spirit is present to give you revelation and to do the necessary spiritual work in your heart and to help you obey the Word of God. The People of God means the Body of Christ. These are people who are anointed in the Holy Spirit and spiritual gifts and can minister to you and help you. Sometimes the People of God are not needed, but other times the People of God are needed to bring the love, power, and revelation of God into your. These three tools are the basic weapons for change, deliverance, and healing.

There is the Word of God. The first way to deal with bad fruit (and many times this will be sufficient) is to obey the Word of God. We should not be deceived by just hearing and reading the Word of God and then not obeying it (James 1:19-25). The Bible

---

1- Whenever you are oppressed, you need to get the yoke broken off of you, even if it keeps coming back. This is because, if you do not get it broken off, this yoke of oppression will end up destroying you emotionally, even your very life.

# Chapter 11

# The Search for Endurance

We live in a world of tribulation, with suffering, hardship, afflictions, and trials, with evil being ever present, and so we have a need for endurance so that we are able to keep on living life and to live it victoriously. Life is difficult. Life is an endurance race and not a sprint. This is especially true for the Christian life. Endurance is a key quality for living the Christian life (2Pet 1:6), and any good systematic theology book will have a chapter or section on the importance of endurance for the saints of God.

What is endurance? Some synonyms for endurance are persistence, keeping on, holding on, patience, fortitude, continuance, steadfastness (standing fast), and perseverance. Perseverance will be used as the primary synonym for endurance. Perseverance was almost chosen as the title word for this chapter because my three favorite Bible translations (NKJV, NIV, NASB) use this word in Romans 5:3-4 (a key passage of Scripture for this chapter). However, endurance was chosen instead because I have found that people are able to define endurance better than perseverance and endurance is more commonly used than perseverance in our society today.

Endurance can be defined in many ways, but the basic idea is going through what is difficult without quitting or working toward a goal until it is completed. Endurance is having the resolve and determination to keep on going despite obstacles in one's way. Endurance is having the strength, firmness, toughness, fortitude, and courage to not quit when confronted with trials and tribulation. Endurance is remaining and standing one's ground and not fleeing in the face of trouble. Endurance is the willingness to abide under and to bear up under a difficult situation. Endurance is not surrendering to circumstances and not succumbing to events. Endurance is sowing until you reap a harvest. Endurance is having patience and faith during trouble without complaining or despairing. Endurance is the outward expression of hope during affliction. Endurance is to continue steadfastly on a course of action or to remain set in purpose or to tenaciously pursue a goal that requires much time and effort or has obstacles and adversity to overcome. Endurance is remaining true to your values and what you believe. Endurance is lasting until the end.

When endurance is defined with God and salvation in Jesus Christ in view, endurance is loving God and following Jesus to the very end. Endurance is standing steadfast and unwavering against wickedness, injustice, a hostile world, and the kingdom of darkness while confidently waiting for the fulfillment of one's redemption and the kingdom of God. Endurance is going through persecution and remaining true to God, righteousness, and the Word of God (Matt 10:28). Endurance is the attitude that looks through tribulation and suffering to find meaning in God and to look not to oneself but to God for strength. Endurance is a key quality for salvation, for Jesus said, "But he who endures to the end will be saved" (Matt 24:13, NKJV).

We need endurance to live life, especially the Christian life. The Christian life is described as a race, a marathon race, and we are exhorted to run the race to win (1Cor 9:24-27, Gal 2:2, 5:7, Phi 2:16, 3:14, 2Tim 2:5-7, 4:7-8, Heb 12:1, Acts 20:24). The Christian life is described as a fight, like a boxing or wrestling match, and we are exhorted to fight the good fight of faith (1Cor 9:26, 1Tim 1:18, 6:12, 2Tim 4:7, Col 4:12). The Christian life is described as warfare, warfare with the flesh, the world, and the kingdom of darkness, and we are exhorted to put on the armor of God and stand against the schemes of the evil one (Matt 6:13, Rom 7:23, 13:12, 1Cor 16:13, 2Cor 6:7, 10:4 Eph 6:10-19, 2Tim 1:14, 2:3-4, Heb 4:12, 1Pet 5:8-9, Rev 12:11). It takes endurance to run a marathon race and to box or wrestle and to fight a war. Thus, we must learn endurance to live the Christian life.

We also need endurance to do a great work, especially if it is the work of God. Whenever you do a great work, there will be tribulation, especially if you are doing the will of God. Nehemiah did a great work for God. He was inspired to rebuild the walls of Jerusalem and he found favor with God and the king to accomplish this task. This was a great work of God, but there was also great

Chapter 12

# The Search for God

The search for God has been saved for the last chapter, although, as we have seen, the search for God is really at the heart of every search that we pursue in life, for if we want to find fulfillment in life, we must know God and His ways. There is a real search for God whether we see it or not. We have been created by God and are created in the image of God and were created to have relationship with God. This is why there is a desire within you to know God and why God must be the center and foundation for your life if you wish to find lasting fulfillment.

However, although we may have a desire to know God, we do not always seek God or seek God in truth and spirit. God pursues us, but we do not always pursue God. Relationship with God, of course, was broken at the beginning when man and woman listened to the father of lies and wanted to be their own gods. Since this time God has pursued man and woman as a lover pursues a beloved, making covenants with those who had a heart to have true relationship with Him. Through this line of people who wanted relationship with God, God birthed a people of His own through Abraham and Sarah and then made a covenant through Moses with their descendants, creating the nation of Israel.

This chosen people would be the means for bringing the Messiah or Christ ("the anointed One") into the world. The Messiah would deliver us from sin and the kingdom of darkness through His death on the cross and resurrection from the dead. This Messiah, the Son of Man and the Son of God, is Jesus Christ, and it is through faith in Him as Savior and Lord that we are reconciled to God and can have true relationship with God.

However, even when one has received Jesus Christ, we still do not live with God face to face in this present age, for the kingdom of God has not yet been established upon the earth. You will see

God face to face when you enter heaven or see the second coming of Jesus Christ, whichever comes first for you. When you see God face to face, then your search for God will end and you will find complete and lasting fulfillment.

In one sense the search for God ends by receiving Jesus Christ as one's Savior and Lord, but in another sense it only begins with Christ. Even though God is in your heart through the Holy Spirit and God is right beside you and always with you, there is still a search for God. There is a search for God to know Him better and to know His will and purposes and to dwell in His glory presence. This searching for God is in essence seeking God (which is the biblical expression). The search for God is seeking God.

Some people do not like the expression "seeking God", believing that we do not need to seek God because God is already with us through Jesus Christ and we are supposed to walk in the Spirit instead of seeking God. However, seeking God is a common theme in the Bible and is used to express the desire to be in the presence of God and to know God and His ways better and to know the will of God. Whether it is getting back to God or having greater fellowship with God. God wants us to seek Him all the time. The Bible says,

"Those who know your name will trust in you, for you, Lord, have never forsaken those who seek you" (Psalm 9:10, NIV; cf. Psalm 24:3-6, 27:4,8, 34:10, 40:16; Deut 4:29, 1Chr 28:9, 2Chr 7:14, 11:16, 14:4,7, 15:2, 26:5, Prov 8:17, 28:5, Jer 29:11-14a).

"When You said, 'Seek My face,' my heart said to You, "Your face, Lord, I will seek" (Psalm 27:8, NKJV; cf. Hosea 10:12).

"Look to the Lord and his strength; seek his face always" (Psalm 105:4, NIV; cf. Isa 55:6, Dan 9:3, Amos 5:4-6, Zeph 2:3).

"Blessed are they who keep his statutes and seek him with all their heart" (Psalm 119:2, NIV, see 119:1-11).

"But seek first the kingdom of God and His righteousness, and all these things shall be added unto you" (Matt 6:33, NKJV; cf. Matt 7:7-11, Luke 11:9-13, 12:31, Acts 17:26-27).

www.ingramcontent.com/pod-product-compliance
Lightning Source LLC
Chambersburg PA
CBHW070704290526
45790CB00001B/439